SELF-HELP _or_ SELF-DESTRUCTION?

SELF-HELP
_or_ SELF-
DESTRUCTION?

DR. CHRIS THURMAN

A
JANET
THOMA
BOOK

THOMAS NELSON PUBLISHERS
Nashville • Atlanta • London • Vancouver

To contact Dr. Thurman about hosting one of his seminars, please call the Center for Marriage and Family Intimacy at 1-800-881-8008.

Published in Nashville, Tennessee, by Thomas Nelson, Inc., Publishers, and distributed in Canada by Word Communications, Ltd., Richmond, British Columbia.

The Bible version used in this publication is THE NEW KING JAMES VERSION. Copyright © 1979, 1980, 1982, 1990, Thomas Nelson, Inc., Publishers.

Library of Congress Cataloging-in-Publication Data

Thurman, Chris.
    Self-help or self-destruction? : pop psychology's most damaging myths and how to keep them from ruining your life / Chris Thurman.
        p.   cm.
    "A Janet Thoma book."
    Includes bibliographical references.
    ISBN 0-7852-7787-0
    1. Christianity—Psychology.
2. Psychology and religion.   3. Bible—Psychology.   4. Good and evil.
5. Self-actualization (Psychology)—Religious aspects—Christianity.   I. Title.
BR110.T47   1996
261.5′15—dc20   95–44588
                                  CIP

Printed in the United States of America.
1 2 3 4 5 6 — 01 00 99 98 97 96

This book is dedicated to
those who counsel
and the hurting people
they serve.

"When principles that run against your deepest convictions begin to win the day, then battle is your calling, and peace has become sin; you must, at the price of dearest peace, lay your convictions bare before friend and enemy, with all the fire of your faith."

—Abraham Kuyper
Dutch theologian

CONTENTS

ACKNOWLEDGMENTS

I am deeply indebted to the many people who helped me during the writing of this book. First, my thanks to the staff at Thomas Nelson Publishers, especially Janet Thoma. They have supported me in ways too numerous to count, and I appreciate their hard work and dedication very much.

My sincere thanks to those who reviewed earlier drafts of this book, including Roy Smith, Dave Moore, Bill Lamb, Dr. Fred Lopez, Dr. Steve Thurman, and Vince Ruggiero. Special thanks to Jerry Bridges of The Navigators for taking the time out of his busy schedule to offer feedback. Each of these men provided invaluable input that helped make the book much better.

Whenever I write a book, my family is right there with me. I am so very thankful for their support. Holly, thank you for loving and encouraging me during the lengthy, often frustrating process of writing a book. Matt, Ashley, and Kelly, thank you for being such great kids and for how often you bring a smile to my face.

How can I possibly thank God for all that He has

done for me? Never fully, I know that. As my spiritual eyesight improves, I see more of God's grace than ever before and am overwhelmed by it. I am deeply indebted to God for all that is good about my life, and I hope this book will be a small "Thank You" for everything He has done for me.

Chris Thurman, Ph.D.
Austin, Texas
August 1995

INTRODUCTION

POP
PSYCHOLOGISTS
SAY THE
CRAZIEST THINGS

Imagine, for a moment, that you are living in the year 1928. Let's say you are married and that you and your spouse are the proud parents of a one-year-old boy. Even though he wakes you up two or three times a night, spills juice on your new carpet, and requires 114 diaper changes a day, that little munchkin is the apple of your eye.

Still, you are nervous about your new role. You find yourself battling disturbing thoughts and feelings each day. Will you be up to the task of raising the little guy properly? You share your concerns with trusted friends, hoping they have some insights into how to raise children properly. They suggest everything from compassion to castor oil. Some of what they say helps, but you still feel anxious. So, you keep sharing your fears with anyone who will listen, hoping that someone will have some helpful ideas.

One day, you are at the local bookstore and you overhear two people talking excitedly about a new book entitled *Psychological Care of Infant and Child* by Dr. John B. Watson (this part is not make-believe; the book and the author are real). Dr. Watson, you discover, is one of the leading psychologists in the world and a highly respected expert on how to raise kids. His new book is hailed by *Atlantic Monthly* magazine as "a godsend to parents" and by *Parents' Magazine* as a book that ought to be "on every intelligent mother's shelf."[1] You enthusiastically purchase a copy, believing you have finally found the answers to all the challenges of raising a happy, well-adjusted child.

You rush home, eager to gain all the insights that Dr. Watson's book has to offer concerning how to make your one-year-old into a successful person. You envision him being sworn in as president of the United States or awarded the Nobel Prize. During his acceptance speech, of course, he gives you complete credit for his becoming the wonderful person he turned out to be. As you read Dr. Watson's book, you come to the following paragraph:

> There is a sensible way of treating children. Treat them as though they were young adults. Dress them,

bathe them with care and circumspection. Let your behavior always be objective and kindly firm. Never hug and kiss them, never let them sit in your lap. If you must, kiss them once on the forehead when they say good night. Shake hands with them in the morning. Give them a pat on the head if they have made an extraordinarily good job of a difficult task.[2]

You are somewhat surprised as you read this. It doesn't reflect how you were raised, and it does not fit with your own common sense about how best to raise a child. Yet, believing that Dr. Watson must know what he is talking about (after all, he is one of the leading psychologists in the world), you do exactly as he says. You hold back from hugging and kissing your one-year-old. You allow yourself to kiss him only at night before he falls asleep and only on the forehead. You never let him cuddle up in your lap. You shake his hand when he wakes up every morning, and you pat him on the head when he does something especially well.

You keep reading Dr. Watson's book, feeling a little uneasy but still delighted to have such expert guidance. Then, you come to the following passage:

If you haven't a nurse and cannot leave the child, put it out in the backyard a large part of the day. Build a fence around the yard so that you are sure no harm can come to it. Do this from the time it is born.

When the child can crawl, give it a sandpile and be sure to dig some small holes in the yard so it has to crawl in and out of them. Let it learn to overcome difficulties almost from the moment of birth. The child should learn to conquer difficulties away from your watchful eye. No child should get commendation and notice and petting every time it does something it ought to be doing anyway. If your heart is too tender and you must watch the child, make yourself a peephole so that you can see it without being seen, or use a periscope.[3]

Now your reservations about Dr. Watson and his advice grow even stronger. "Put him out in the back-yard most of the day? Dig holes for him to crawl in and out of? Watch him with a periscope?" But you also think, *Who am I to doubt this highly respected expert? Thousands of people are buying his book, and well-respected magazines are raving about it.*

You have a fence put up so the little tyke can't escape from the backyard. You dutifully get a shovel out of the garage and begin to dig holes in the back-yard. While digging, you look next door and feel com-forted by the fact that Mr. and Mrs. Jones, proud parents of a little girl, are digging holes in their back-yard as well. Everyone, it seems, is on the Watson bandwagon. You buy yourself a periscope so that you can watch your child without being seen.

Your child spends most every day, rain or shine,

out in the backyard, playing in the sand, going in and out of those holes. You realize you dug one hole too deep when he disappears altogether and can't get out, a minor glitch that can easily be corrected with some fill dirt. Overall, you are quite satisfied with all you have done to comply with Dr. Watson's instructions, and you sit back, trusting that your child is headed toward becoming president or a Nobel Prize winner or a brain surgeon.

All this seems pretty absurd, doesn't it? As you read Dr. Watson's words of wisdom on raising kids from the year 1928, didn't you say to yourself, "What kind of fool would follow that type of advice?"

Well, apparently there were a lot of "fools" back in 1928 and the years that followed, because more than 100,000 copies of Dr. Watson's *Psychological Care of Infant and Child* were sold. Untold thousands were influenced by what he had to say, raising their children under the guidance of his "expert" authority. Can you imagine the results of following his advice?

To be fair, the statements I quoted from Dr. Watson's book do not represent all that he had to say on how to raise kids. Nor did his book necessarily represent the best that psychology had to offer at the time. Yet, let me ask you two simple questions. First, do you think the advice we are getting from some psychological experts today is any better than what Dr. Watson offered in 1928, whether the topic is raising kids, building self-esteem, having a great marriage, being assertive, or overcoming depression? Second, are we being any less foolish in believing and following what they offer?

I believe the answer to those two questions is a resounding "No!" I am convinced that what far too many psychological experts teach, while well-intentioned, is actually damaging to your emotional and spiritual health. The purpose of this book is to examine some of the most destructive teachings that have come from these experts via the popular books they write. While I know that millions of people have been genuinely helped by pop psychology books, I hope to show you that mixed in with their helpful insights are teachings that are anything but helpful. I also plan to offer you something better than what these books do.

First, I want to tell you about the route I traveled that led me to write this book.

· · · · · · · · · · · ·

On Becoming a Psychologist and (Gulp) a Self-Help Author

My interest in becoming a psychologist began when I was fairly young. At the age of fourteen, I wrote a letter to the American Psychological Association (APA) asking for information on how to become a psychologist. They were glad to send me literature describing the various areas of psychology, the job outlook for each, and the level of training required. My writing the APA at an age when most adolescents are worried about the zits on their faces and getting dates (I worried about both) reflected an interest in helping people with personal problems, a desire to understand myself better, and a belief that psychology was the field to go into if I wanted to do both.

During high school, I never wavered in my desire to become a psychologist, and I majored in psychology in college. The first class I took, Introduction to Psychology, was an eye-opening experience. I remember walking into class the first day to find six hundred students crammed into a large auditorium. My entire senior class in high school had been that size! I sat down, wondering what I had gotten myself into. My apprehension only worsened when the professor walked in. He was quite old, lectured in a barely audible monotone, and gave multiple-choice exams that never seemed to have any correct answers among the choices. The class did little to heighten my interest in psychology.

I went on to take classes in personality (because I needed one), abnormal psychology (to figure out my friends), statistics (to learn how to lie with numbers), child psychology (to understand my "inner child"), experimental psychology (to better understand rats), and learning theory (to see why I wasn't learning anything in college). All were interesting for the most part, some more relevant to my becoming a counselor than others. By the grace of God, I finished all of my course work and graduated with a degree in psychology in four years.

Somewhere along the way it dawned on me that an undergraduate degree in psychology was pretty useless (about eight billion people have one); graduate school was going to be a must. So, off I went to earn master's and doctoral degrees in counseling psychology. I studied under a number of professors for whom I developed a great deal of respect, and I was fortunate to meet and become friends with numerous fellow students. It was a challenging and exciting time.

During the years I spent preparing to become a psychologist (all ten of them), I put a great deal of faith in what I was taught. I studied the most popular approaches in the counseling field (it has been estimated that there are more than 250 different counseling approaches), believing that in doing so I would find the best answers to people's problems. In spite of the helpful insights, what I learned was more often a source of confusion than of clarity.

Many of the counseling approaches were at odds with each other, and all of them left out critically important aspects of why we human beings are the way we are and why we develop the problems that we do. More than seventy years ago, medical historian F. H. Garrison noted, "Whenever many different remedies are used for a disease, it usually means that we know very little about the disease." I believe Garrison's comment applies not only to the field of medicine, but to the field of psychology, as well.

It wasn't until I had been out of school for a number of years that it began to dawn on me (I'm a little slow) that some—maybe a lot—of what I had been taught was simply not valid. I began to read books that were critical of psychotherapy and popular psychology in general (something I don't remember being encouraged to do during my training), and my concerns grew.

I visited bookstores and saw all the books that lined the shelves of the self-help/psychology section. The various theories and concepts I studied during school were right there in pop psychology form, available for public consumption. More than a few of these books seemed to promise readers psychological nirvana, sometimes in thirty days or less. From my own training and clinical experience, I knew that some of these books were passing along as psychological "truths" ideas that were, and still are, unproven.

Another part of the route I traveled in coming to write this book involved becoming a self-help author myself. I had been counseling others for about six years when the opportunity to write my first book came along. I jumped at the chance without really thinking much about it. I believed I had something important to say that would genuinely help people (what author doesn't?), and I did my dead-level best to say it as well as I could. The result, *The Lies We*

Believe, published in 1989 and has gone on to sell more than 100,000 copies. Since then, I have authored or coauthored a number of other books.

The fact that I have written self-help books and that more than a few people have actually been influenced by them is another reason for the concern that I have about these books in general. After all, who am I to presume to tell people how to live their lives? Why should anyone put their trust in me or any self-help author?

I believe the answer is pretty simple: People put their trust in us because they need expert advice and we claim to be experts. To ensure that we are seen as experts, we trot out our Ph.D.'s or M.D.'s (or whatever degrees we have), along with all of our life experiences, and say, "Trust me, I know what I am talking about." We do all we can to convince readers that what we have to say is worth living their lives by. That scares me, though, and I hope it scares you. More often than not what we self-help authors are offering for public consumption is "guesswork fueled by personal biases and masked by scientific jargon."[4] This isn't being harsh; it is just being honest.

Please don't interpret this as me trying to tell you that pop psychology authors don't know anything. Of course they do. Sometimes they know a great deal. But how many self-help authors are willing to tell you, "What I *don't* know is so much greater than what I *do* know"? How many are willing to tell you, "What

I am passing along as 'truth' is often based on unsubstantiated theory"? From what I have read, not many.

I am greatly concerned about how pop psychology authors presume to be the new "Solomons," dispensing their wisdom to us. I am concerned about how some authors want to turn us into helpless little children while still others want to turn us into all-powerful giants. I am concerned about how they teach that our problems are mostly external rather than internal. I am concerned about how some teach that you can change almost overnight, while others seem to teach that it will take forever to change—as if this can be predicted. I am concerned about how many authors encourage us to focus on how badly we have been treated rather than encouraging us to look at how badly we have treated others. I am concerned about how they often define success in terms of personal happiness, financial wealth, or personal power instead of other criteria such as love for others, self-control, and humility. I am especially bothered by the lip service many in self-help psychology give to spiritual matters in people's lives and how often they teach things that either leave God out altogether or encourage people to become their own little gods.

· · · · · · · · · · ·

Some Final Thoughts

In criticizing what certain pop psychology authors teach, I am not judging them personally. I know there is a fine line here, but I hope to honor it. I wouldn't presume to know the personal characters or motives of the authors whose writings I will examine. So, as you read through this book, please keep in mind that I am criticizing what they *say,* not who they *are.*

I am not recommending that you "throw the baby out with the bathwater" either. To use a food analogy, I am writing this book not to tell you to quit eating but to tell you which foods are bad for your health and which foods are good for you.

Isn't it arrogant for me to think that I am somehow smarter or more insightful than all these people? The fact of the matter is that many of the writers whose works I will critique are much more intelligent and more insightful than I am.

So, why listen to me? The truth is, I don't want you to listen to me. I am writing this book from the point of view that there is one author who is much smarter, wiser, and more insightful than all the rest of us put together. He has authored sixty-six books that have been put into one single collection, and that collection is at the very top of the best-seller list year in and year out. Yet, this author has never appeared on Oprah, Phil, or Geraldo (thank goodness!). The author I am referring to is God, and the sixty-six books He wrote are called the Bible.

I believe the Bible explains reality better than any other book, and it is *the* authoritative text on who we are, why we are here, and how we can live life fully.

The author of the Bible, unlike those of us who write self-help personal-growth books, knows *everything* there is to know about His subject and *perfectly* practices what He teaches. There is no book like the Bible and no author like God.

If you don't put much stock in God or the Bible, I ask you to let me show you some of what the Bible teaches and compare that with certain self-help books. Then, I want you to ask yourself, "Which view fits reality better, makes more sense, and would be more helpful if implemented in my life?"

I have a challenge, as well, for those of you who believe in the Bible. I want you to be as honest as you can about how much you may have bought into what pop psychology often teaches. Sadly, many of us believe the destructive myths propagated in self-help books. Far too often, we are "in the world and of it" when it comes to how we think and act. I want you to entertain that unpleasant possibility and see "if the shoe fits."

Let me close this introduction with a story that I hope will drive home what I want to say in this book. When my wife, Holly, was in college, she had some car problems. She turned to some friends for advice, and one of them suggested that her car might need some water. So Holly got some water, raised the hood, spotted the place where she thought the water went, opened it up, and proceeded to pour away.

Turns out that Holly poured the water where the

oil goes. Now, car engines refuse to work when you do that to them. Holly had to have all the water and oil drained out of her engine and new oil put back in.

I hope to demonstrate that accepting the advice being offered in many pop psychology books is like putting water where the oil goes in a car engine. Many of these authors assume they are offering us high-quality oil for our souls, but they frequently offer water instead. When we accept what they say, our souls sputter through life. Sometimes, our souls stop altogether.

Truth is the only proper lubricant for our souls. When we experience truth deeply, we run pretty smoothly. Life, of course, will still put painful bumps, potholes, and detours in our way, but our lives will be healthy because truth is keeping everything running. As much as possible, we need to drain the false teachings we have adopted out of our souls and put the truth in so we can become who we were truly meant to be.

What are the false teachings from pop psychology that are the most destructive, and what does the Bible have to say about them? Does the Bible offer us hope for a healthy, mature, and meaningful life beyond what pop psychology offers? Keep reading.

CHAPTER 1

Pop psychology myth #1:

PEOPLE ARE BASICALLY GOOD

You may be familiar with Erik and Lyle Menendez, two brothers who are accused of brutally killing their wealthy parents. Erik and Lyle openly admit having committed the murders but claim they did so in self-defense. They contend that their father had a history of abusing them and that he would have ultimately killed them both. The case has sent a shudder or two up the spines of many parents.

What ought to scare us even more is what their lawyer, Leslie Abramson, said about one of the boys: "Erik Menendez is a good person who did a bad thing." In other words, Erik is basically a fine fellow; he just blew his parents away while they were eating ice cream and watching television because they had created such a painful and life-threatening environment for him.

Now, I'll be the first to agree that some parents do create very painful and even life-threatening environments for their children. I have heard far too many of those kinds of stories to think otherwise. But, isn't it possible that Erik Menendez is a bad person who found a way to use his painful past as an excuse to murder his parents, inherit their wealth, and live a life of pleasure?

More than a few pop psychologists share Ms. Abramson's positive view of people's nature. Open up most pop psychology books on personal growth, and you will find that they teach, "People are, by nature, basically good." As common as this view is, I believe it is one of the most destructive myths taught in pop psychology. Let me give you some examples of best-selling authors who teach this myth.

Take Melody Beattie, author of the best-seller *Codependent No More* (more than three million copies sold), for instance. After defining a codependent as "one who has let another person's behavior affect him or her, and who is obsessed with controlling that person's behavior" (all of us on the planet, basically) and noting that most codependents "suffer from that vague but penetrating affliction, low self-worth," Beattie suggests we must quit torturing ourselves and try to raise our view of ourselves. How, you ask? Let's allow Beattie to answer that:

> Right now, we can give ourselves a big emotional and mental hug. We are okay. It's wonderful to be who we are. Our thoughts are okay. Our feelings are appropriate. We're right where we're supposed to be today, this moment. There is nothing wrong with us. There is nothing fundamentally wrong with us.[1]

Notice what Beattie believes to be central to solving a self-esteem problem: believing "there is nothing wrong with us. There is nothing fundamentally wrong with us." Must be that the more you tell yourself something, the truer it becomes. Anyway, no matter what you are struggling with or how messed up you may be or how bad a shape the world is in, Beattie wants all of us to know that we are just fine as we are. In other words, *we are basically good*.

Peter McWilliams, in his best-seller *Life 101*, actually has a brief section entitled, "Are human beings fundamentally good or fundamentally evil?" He not only answers the question but tells us why he believes what he does:

> My answer: good. My proof? I could quote philosophers, psychologists, and poets, but then those who believe humans are fundamentally evil can quote just as many philosophers, psychologists, and

poets. My proof, such as it is, is a simple one. It returns to the source of human life: an infant. When you look into the eyes of an infant, what do you see? I've looked into a few, and I have yet to see fundamental evil radiating from a baby's eyes. There seems to be purity, joy, brightness, splendor, sparkle, marvel, happiness—you know: good.[2]

McWilliams must not have any kids. When I look into a child's eyes, I see a pleasure-seeking, pain-avoiding, self-absorbed guided missile. I see someone who wants what he wants, when he wants it, and who will scream to high heaven if you don't deliver the goods immediately. I love children (I have three of them myself), and I do see positive qualities in them at birth. But I don't see fundamental goodness radiating from their eyes as McWilliams does.

I was up late one night working on this book when I happened to catch an episode of *The Dennis Prager Show.* The topic for the show was "Are people basically good?" Strangely enough, Dennis Prager also used infants to answer the question, but his answer was diametrically opposed to that of Peter McWilliams. Here is what Prager had to say:

I am told, "Dennis, what do you mean people aren't basically good? Look at babies. Aren't they beautiful, adorable, innocent?" Well, the answer is, "Yes, babies are beautiful, adorable, and innocent. However, they are also the ultimate in selfishness."[3]

Prager went on to play a humorous videotape he had made of what a baby would say if it could speak: "I want milk. I want milk. I want to lie down and go to sleep. Oh, I don't know what I want, but if you don't give it to me, I'll ruin your life." If babies were inherently good, he suggests, they would say something like "Go ahead, Mommy, get some rest. You could really use it. My diaper is rather full, but don't you worry." After making his point that babies are not this way, he states:

> Now in the history of humanity, no baby has ever been born that has actually thought, "Gee, I think I will suppress my urge to vomit or cry or poop because Mommy hasn't had enough sleep." The baby is made—we start out totally preoccupied with ourselves. OK, that's the baby. Babies, again, not good, but not bad, but certainly don't start out good.[4]

I think Prager has it half right. He says that babies (and people in general) aren't basically good, but he can't bring himself to say they are basically bad. After noting that we begin life "the ultimate in selfishness," he still wants to camp on the idea that we are neither basically good nor basically bad. But how can we begin life completely self-centered and focused only on our own needs as Prager suggests and *not* be inherently bad?

Finally, one of the world's most famous psychologists, Abraham Maslow, joins the fray on this issue by suggesting that not only are we not intrinsically bad but, at worst, we are neutral and most probably good. In his book, *Toward a Psychology of Being,* he states:

> The inner nature, as much as we know of it so far, seems not to be intrinsically evil but rather neutral or positively "good." . . . Since this inner nature is good or neutral rather than bad, it is best to bring it out and to encourage it rather than to suppress it. If it is permitted to guide our life, we grow healthy, fruitful, and happy.[5]

We are inherently good, and, if we allow our inherent goodness to "guide our life," we become "healthy, fruitful, and happy"? I, for one, would love to see someone prove that. Abraham Maslow never did, even though he was convinced it was true. Yet, even Maslow, as positive as he is about our nature, goes on to make a rather interesting admission:

> There are certainly good and strong and successful men in the world . . . But it also remains true that there are so few of them, even though there could be so many more, and that they are often badly treated by their fellows. So this too must be studied, this fear of human goodness and greatness, this lack of knowledge of how to be good and strong, this

inability to turn one's anger into productive activities, this fear of maturing, this fear of feeling virtuous, self-loving, love-worthy, respect-worthy. Especially we must learn how to transcend our foolish tendency to let our compassion for the weak generate hatred for the strong.[6]

It seems like Maslow wants to argue that humans are basically good, then turn right around and say the very things that prove they are not. If Maslow is right, and we humans are "neutral" or "positively good," why is it that there are so few people who are really good?

If people are basically good, wouldn't we find at least one culture somewhere on the planet that is full of good people and relatively free from corruption? Seems to me that those who suggest we are basically good want to argue out of both sides of their mouth: "People are basically good, but there are hardly any good people in the world and the world is such a mess."

This whole issue of whether or not people are basically good is getting another examination in the O. J. Simpson case. It seems that if "regular" people are basically good, then famous people are even "gooder." Few people, at first, could believe that O. J. Simpson might have killed his ex-wife, Nicole, and Ronald Goldman. Why? Because of the "People are basically good" myth and its first cousin, the "Talented, beautiful, powerful, and wealthy people are even more inherently good" myth. O. J. Simpson won the Heisman Trophy, is in the NFL Hall of Fame, has starred in motion pictures, and was a national spokesman with Arnold Palmer for Hertz rental cars. He is attractive, charming, and wealthy. Surely he couldn't have done such a horrible thing.

I am not saying O. J. Simpson killed Nicole Brown and Ronald Goldman. We don't know if he did, and we may never know. I'm just pointing out that we tend to be doubly shocked when we hear about a case like this. Wrongdoing by anyone strikes us as abnormal or unusual. It is as if we are collectively saying, "People, especially famous ones, don't really act that way, do they?" Well, yes, Virginia, they do. Our newspapers and televisions only report the tip of the iceberg—not a very pleasant thought, but a lot closer to reality than the idea that wrongdoing is a freak of human nature.

Let me move this discussion closer to home. In arguing against the idea that people are basically good, I personally *would not* use the more dramatic examples of human evil like Nazi concentration camps or Cambodian killing fields. It isn't the horrific, "made for television" things people do that prove we are not fundamentally good. I believe it is the small, often unnoticeable, things we do moment by moment.

Think about your own life. Do you ever go

through a single day without doing things that are immoral, illegal, unethical, or just plain selfish? Before you answer, think about whether or not you speed on the highway, tell "little white lies" to avoid unpleasant situations, do "nice" things because you want approval, gossip about people behind their backs, or get upset when things don't go the way you want them to. These more common, daily actions are the true evidence that none of us are basically good.

Why make such a fuss over the myth "People are basically good"? I believe this myth is destroying us individually and as a culture in two very frightening ways.

First, this myth causes us to downplay the moral seriousness of the wrong we do. For example, Erik Menendez's lawyer referred to what he did as a "bad thing." Ms. Abramson, excuse me for objecting, but eating too much pepperoni pizza and using up two spaces when you park your car at the mall are "bad" things. What Erik did wasn't bad, it was evil. When we believe the myth that people are basically good, our moral measuring stick disintegrates. Evil actions end up being viewed as "bad," and bad actions end up being viewed as "okay."

Second, the myth "People are basically good" prompts us to search for external reasons to justify the things people do. ("Yes, she drowned her two kids in the lake, but her boyfriend had rejected her.") If I am basically good, when I do something bad it isn't the "real" me. Something in my environment must be to blame, not something inside me. Charles Colson puts it this way:

> This myth [that mankind is basically good] deludes people into thinking that they are always victims, never villains; always deprived, never depraved. It dismisses responsibility as the teaching of a darker age. It can excuse any crime, because it can always blame something else—a sickness of our society or a sickness of the mind.[7]

There is something agreeable about being told that our natural moral "bent" is positive rather than negative. Yet, while it certainly feels good to be told that, it isn't really good for us. John Calvin, in his classic, *Institutes of the Christian Religion,* hit this right on the head when he said:

> In every age, he who is most forward in extolling the excellence of human nature is received with the loudest applause. But . . . it does nothing more than fascinate by its sweetness and, at the same time, so delude as to drown in perdition all who assent to it.[8]

The sweetness of this myth ultimately leaves a bitter result in our lives and in our culture. Let's turn away from the "sweetness" of pop psychology's view of man's nature to see what the Bible has to say about us.

. . . .

The Biblical View of Man's Nature

Strap on your seat belt, because this ride through Scripture is going to get pretty rough. Most in theological circles would agree that the Bible teaches two things related to man's nature: original sin and total depravity. Let's look at both.

Original sin basically means that ever since Adam and Eve committed the first sin, the human race has been born morally corrupt. All of us are born "in Adam" and begin life in a state of sinfulness. *The Westminster Confession of Faith* describes our situation clearly:

> By this sin they fell from their original righteousness and communion with God, and so became dead in sin, wholly defiled in all parts and faculties of soul and body. They being the root of all mankind, the guilt of this sin was imputed, and the same death in sin, and corrupted nature, conveyed to all their posterity descending from them by ordinary generation. From this original corruption, whereby we are utterly indisposed, disabled, and made opposite to all good, and wholly inclined to all evil, do proceed all actual transgressions.[9]

In other words, you and I are a mess at the core of our being from the very start of our lives. Or, as David puts it in Psalm 51:5, "Behold, I was brought forth in iniquity, / And in sin my mother conceived me." We are not sinners because we sin. We sin because we are, by nature, sinners. A bent toward sin (missing the moral mark) is at the very foundation of who we are. Not good news, is it? This is certainly at odds with pop psychology's notion that we are neutral or good from birth. These authors see "sin" (not that they would call it by that name) as something abnormal or peripheral to our nature.

Well, how about some more good news? Not only are we born in sin, but we suffer from something called "total depravity." Nothing about a human being escapes the taint of sin. Our minds, wills, emotions, and bodies are all flawed. If you are a perfectionist, the whole notion of total depravity is quite a blow because it means *nothing* about you can ever be perfect, no matter how hard you try to make it so.

Total depravity is different from something called "utter depravity," though. Utter depravity means that a person acts as wickedly as he or she possibly can, something that few people ever do. Total depravity means that every dimension of who you are is affected by sin, whereas utter depravity means that you are acting as horribly as you possibly can across all the dimensions of your life.

The biblical teachings on original sin and total depravity, when taken together, are in direct opposition to the teachings of many pop psychology books. Verses like "All have sinned and fall short of the glory of God"[10] and "The works of the flesh are evident, which are: adultery, fornication, uncleanness, lewdness, idolatry, sorcery, hatred, contentions, jealousies, outbursts of wrath, selfish ambitions, dissensions, heresies, envy, murders, drunkenness, revelries, and the like"[11] teach that sin is at the center of who we are and messes up everything we think, feel, and do.

The biblical view of man's nature fits the reality of the world much better than the myth that people are basically good. When we look as honestly as we can into our own souls and the souls of others, we see more selfishness, arrogance, manipulation, and judgmentalness than selflessness, forgiveness, humility, grace, and respect. It isn't that we humans don't do kind, thoughtful, or unselfish things; it's just that these acts are never Ivory soap pure and are so few and far between.

How does what the Bible teaches help us? Well, if you and I step out on the planet each day with a sense of conviction about the depth of sin in our souls and the pervasive impact it has on our lives, I think we end up experiencing:

- a clearer sense that our problems are more internal than external

- a true sorrow and humility about our sins that leads to change on our part
- a deeper motivation to focus on and do good
- a greater sense of accountability to God and others He might use in our lives to mature us.

Let me make this point from a marital perspective. If I believe that I am basically a good person, I will tend to see my own actions toward my wife, Holly, from that perspective. The things I do and say will seem more innocent and justifiable to me, and I will have a harder time understanding why she is so upset over my actions at times. "Why is she getting so bent out of shape? All I did was . . ." and "I'm a good guy. Why doesn't she cut me some slack?" will be my reactions to her grievances.

If, on the other hand, I understand the depth of my "fallenness" as a human being, I will enter my marriage (and everything else I do) with a greater sense of humility and brokenness. When Holly is upset with me, I won't be surprised by the possibility that my actions may be off base, and I won't feel such a strong need to defend myself against criticism. I am more likely to admit what I have done and make an effort to change. And I will make myself more accountable to God, my wife, and others.

Please don't hear this as my saying that you should always see yourself as the problem any time someone is upset with you or something goes wrong. I am just saying that a greater honesty about our own sinfulness helps us to be healthier, more mature people.

Sin, as a concept, has gone out of style. Dr. Karl Menninger, one of our country's most well-respected psychiatrists, noted this problem in 1973 in his book, *Whatever Became of Sin?* He wrote, "In all the laments and reproaches made by our seers and prophets, one misses any mention of 'sin,' a word which used to be a veritable watchword of prophets. It was a word once in everyone's mind, but now rarely if ever heard."[12]

The word *sin* is mentioned *even less* today than it was more than twenty years ago when Dr. Menninger penned those words. Why? Is it because we are sinning less? No, that's absurd. It is because what we used to call "sin" is now being called "dysfunction," "disease," "addiction," "sickness," or "mistakes." I would much rather be told I have a "disease" or "sickness" than be told I have a problem with sin. Many pop psychology authors seem more than glad to call wrong behavior by names other than "sin" because such euphemizing makes us feel better about ourselves (and—surprise, surprise—sells lots of books).

Yet, when the Bible says, "There is none righteous, no, not one . . . there is none who seeks after God. They have all turned aside; they have together become unprofitable; there is none who does good, no, not one,"[13] it isn't being negative, it is just being honest.

Compared to God's goodness, none of us are "good." God is the standard for goodness, not Mother Theresa or Billy Graham. That is why I hesitated even to say, as I did earlier, that there are so few "good" people in the world. If God is the standard of what goodness is, there are no truly "good" people at all.

When Christ came to earth almost two thousand years ago, he had the most problems with the moral elite of the day, the Pharisees. They dedicated their wholes lives to doing God's commands, and no one could match them when it came to the zeal they had for being righteous. They were the "goodest of the good." Yet, Christ called them a "brood of vipers" and "whitewashed tombs." Why did He have such a negative reaction to the Pharisees?

The Pharisees were practicing an external form of goodness while remaining morally bankrupt inside their hearts. They were so caught up in dotting the moral *i* and crossing the ethical *t,* they had gotten away from honestly facing their depravity and working on internal change. Practicing the do's and avoiding the don'ts had become their god.

Practicing external goodness for public consumption is a common practice today. Don't be fooled into thinking people are basically good just because you can see people doing good. True goodness has only been demonstrated by one person in the history of humankind: Jesus Christ. Compare yourself or anyone you know to Christ, and I think you will find it hard to hang on to the notion that we humans are basically good.

If you don't believe in what the Bible teaches, you may be having a pretty strong negative reaction to all of this, especially the ideas of original sin and total depravity. They are unpleasant notions, and they certainly don't help to make us feel better about ourselves. But I want to ask you to chew on the possibility that sin is, in fact, at the center of your being—not on the periphery—and that it pollutes every aspect of who you are to some degree. Let that humble you, let it bring you to your knees. It will be the best brokenness of your life if it takes you to God for help. God is ready, willing, and able to forgive your sins and give you a brand new start.

If you are a Christian, you have already done this and have become a "new creature" in Christ. Yet, you still war with the old sinful patterns you first developed during your non-Christian years. Even with a new nature, you have a serious daily battle on your hands. These struggles should take you to Christ each day as well, to ask for His help to "fight the good fight" and "finish the race."

Christ did not come to tell you "You're OK." He came to tell you that you're not OK, but deeply loved, that you need radical surgery of the soul, and that He is just the surgeon to do the job. If all of us are "OK," then Christianity is only "take it if you want it" news, not the "good" news that salvation is available to morally "sick" people. We only demean God when we see ourselves as "good," and we end up with much less desire to move in the direction of the standard of goodness that His Son set.

The idea that people are basically good is a belief that tickles our ears and makes us feel good about ourselves, but it is like the Pharisees—a whitewashed tomb that is pretty on the outside but full of death and decay on the inside. It has infiltrated our world on a large scale, helping to create millions of people who see little wrong with what they do and who blame external forces when they do something bad. It has helped to create a world where arrogance and pride are the norm and humility and brokenness are the rarity.

We must stop believing the myth that "People are basically good" and stop teaching it to our children. We need to confront our sinfulness honestly on a daily basis, no matter how painful that will be. Rest assured, though, that facing our sinfulness doesn't mean that we must hate ourselves, condemn ourselves, or think of ourselves as worthless. As we will see in chapters to come, there is a biblical basis for having worth and for loving ourselves.

Are people basically good? That depends on who you listen to. Listen to many pop psychologists, and the answer is a pretty big "Yes." Listen to the God of the universe, and the answer is "No, not compared to

Me." May I suggest that you close the book and think about this issue for a few minutes? Which side of the fence you land on will make all the difference in the world.

CHAPTER 2

Pop psychology myth #2:

YOU NEED MORE SELF-ESTEEM AND SELF-WORTH

Saturday Night Live, the NBC comedy show, used to do a skit with two characters, Hanz and Franz. Hanz and Franz were loosely modeled after Arnold Schwarzeneggar (a world champion bodybuilder and movie star), from their bulked-up physiques to their foreign accents. In the skits, Hanz and Franz would make fun of any guy who was out of shape, calling him a "flabby little girly-man." Their best-known line in each skit was "We're here to pump you up!"

Well, pop psychology and Hanz and Franz have something in common—both are doing all they can to "pump you up." The first pop psychology myth we covered, "People are basically good," is aimed at pumping you up. Related to that teaching is another destructive notion—"You need more self-esteem and self-worth."

Self-esteem and self-worth are central themes in many pop psychology books, which suggest that the reason people are so defeated in life is that they don't feel good about themselves. Some of these books want you to believe that your self-esteem is the most important thing in the world; you should do everything you can to raise it. In this chapter, I want to examine a single book that is representative of many on this topic—*Self-Esteem* (1987) by Matthew McKay and Patrick Fanning.

According to McKay and Fanning, "Self-esteem is essential for psychological survival." They don't really ever define self-esteem in the book, but you get the impression that they see it as how you feel about yourself. The authors seem to be under the impression that you should have high self-esteem, regardless of what you do or have done. They believe that the ultimate destroyer of self-esteem is an internal "pathological critic" who judges us too frequently and too harshly. They suggest we disarm this critic, quit judging ourselves altogether, and learn to accept ourselves as we are. Key to their approach, McKay and Fanning believe that we have to change how we think about ourselves and learn to affirm ourselves more often.

Let's take a brief look at some of the affirmations

McKay and Fanning suggest we tell ourselves in order to enhance our sense of worth and esteem:

1. *"I am worthwhile because I breathe and feel and am aware."*[1]

Does this seem like much of a basis for personal worth? Doesn't a sewer rat then have as much worth as we do? And do we stop having worth when we don't breathe for a few seconds? This affirmation is a takeoff on René Descartes' "I think, therefore, I am." McKay and Fannings's version seems to be, "I am, therefore, I am worthwhile."

2. *"I am basically all right as I am."*[2]

Do any of us want Charles Manson telling this to himself? I saw him in an interview on television the other night, and I can promise you he is not all right as he is. He thinks he is God and that his actions in the past were appropriate. I can just see him in his prison cell reading McKay and Fanning's book and saying over and over to himself, "I am basically all right as I am. I am basically all right as I am. I am basically all right as I am." Do you think the parole board is going to buy that idea the next time there is a hearing on whether or not to release him?

Don't all of us need to change some things about ourselves? You are who you are at the moment—there is no doubt about that—but does that make you "all right"? If the Bible is correct, none of us are "all right" as we currently are, and we never will be until we reach a perfect state in heaven.

3. *"It's all right to meet my needs as I see fit."*[3]

Really? What if meeting my needs as I see fit involves doing something that harms another human being? What if meeting my needs as I see fit means stealing from a grocery store because I am hungry? Or killing you in order to take your wallet because I'm out of money? Or cutting in front of you in line because I am in a hurry? Are all those things okay because they meet my needs?

As humans, we certainly have needs, and I personally believe that *wanting* to have those needs met is fine. But getting my needs met "as I see fit" opens a Pandora's box of potential problems. That attitude is one step away from an even more destructive way of thinking: "I'll do whatever it takes to get my needs met, because my needs are the most important thing." Can you imagine a world in which everyone is focused on meeting their own needs as each sees fit?

4. *"Everything I do is an attempt to meet legitimate needs."*[4]

We all have legitimate needs, that's true. And attempting to meet them is fine. But this statement goes a step beyond this and declares that every action we take is an effort to meet legitimate needs. Is that really true? I don't think so. Sometimes we do things because of *illegitimate* needs. Let me give you some examples.

Let's say I rant and rave at waiters because they are slow. Is my need to have everything in life go my way a legitimate or illegitimate need? What if I beat myself up every time I make a mistake? Is my need to be perfect legitimate or illegitimate? What if I get depressed because my wife won't let me tell her how to live her life? Is my need to control her legitimate or illegitimate?

Aren't both legitimate and illegitimate needs usually underneath our actions at times? Like writing this book. On the legitimate side of the coin, I have a need to help you, the reader, avoid destructive teachings. On the illegitimate side of the coin, I have a need to be rich and famous and appear on the *Oprah Winfrey Show*. If any of us waited until our needs were perfectly legitimate before we did anything, we would wait forever. Yet McKay and Fanning seem to be suggesting that illegitimate needs are not underneath the things we do at all. That's nonsense.

5. *"My basic job in life is expanding my awareness."*[5]

When did "expanding my awareness" become my basic job in life? I thought my basic job in life was to love God with all my heart, mind, and soul and to love my neighbor as myself. Do I really want to expand my awareness about certain things in life, like knowing more about all the kinds of evil men do?

I agree that ignorance about ourselves is not bliss, but I sure wish McKay and Fanning would do a better job of defining "expanding my awareness." Left undefined, it opens up the door for doing whatever I want, whenever I want, no matter who might be hurt in the process.

6. *"Today you like yourself more than yesterday, and tomorrow you will like yourself more than today."*[6]

Boy, by the end of my life, I ought to like myself a ton! What if I do something unlikable, though? How do I handle that?

Let's say I spent all day yesterday feeding the poor. Let's say that I spend all day today stealing from the poor. According to McKay and Fanning, I am supposed to like myself more today than yesterday, right? But somehow I have a hard time believing that I should like myself more and more each day, regardless of my behavior.

Let's summarize these self-affirmations before we go on. McKay and Fanning are basically saying:

- We have worth because we exist.
- We are basically all right as we are.
- It is fine to meet our own needs however we see fit.
- Legitimate needs are underneath everything we do.
- The chief goal in life is expanding our self-awareness.
- We need to like ourselves more and more each day.

Have you ever heard more self-serving, narcissistic hogwash in your whole life?

. . . .

The Biblical View of Self-Esteem and Self-Worth

What does the Bible teach about self-esteem and self-worth? I should point out that the words *self-esteem* and *self-worth* are not in the Bible, so I can't offer you biblical definitions of these terms. But I can offer you some insights into how the Bible treats these issues.

First, let me distinguish between "self-esteem" and "self-worth." William James, considered by many to be the father of American psychology, defined self-esteem this way: self-esteem = successes/pretensions. In other words, your self-esteem is a reflection of how you are actually performing (your current "successes") compared to how you think you should be performing (your current "pretensions" or expectations). I believe this is the best way to define self-esteem.

If we accept this definition, a person's self-esteem should actually go up and down each day. Why? Because how we perform and what we expect of ourselves fluctuate from day to day.

Let's say I have the goal ("pretension") of being a fantastic father to my kids (a "100"). On certain days, I'm a pretty good dad (if I do say so myself!). On those days, the ratio of my "successes" to my "pretensions" is, let's say, 95/100, and my self-esteem as a father is pretty high. On other days, though, my performance as a dad is not so good. On those days, the ratio of my "successes" to my "expectations" is downright poor, let's say 65/100, and my self-esteem as a dad is pretty low. The truth of the matter is that my self-esteem as a dad (or husband or psychologist or anything else I do that involves performance) will fluctuate to some degree because my actual performance fluctuates.

Our self-esteem is affected not only by our "success" level each day but also by our expectations. Some days, we expect more out of ourselves; some days, less. For example, last year the Dallas Cowboys' best running back, Emmit Smith, injured his hamstring. When Emmit Smith is healthy, he and his teammates "expect" him to rush for as many as one hundred yards or more a game. When he pulled his hamstring, I don't think anyone in his right mind expected him to rush for even ten yards until he was healthy again. It was appropriate for both Emmit Smith and the Cowboys to lower their expectations.

The same thing is true in life. When we are healthy (physically, emotionally, and spiritually), we can perform better. Even then, our performance will fluctuate some (when Emmit Smith is healthy, he doesn't rush for the same number of yards every game). When we are injured, though, we need to lower our expectations to some degree, accepting the fact that we are not capable of doing as well as we normally could. That isn't making excuses; it's just facing facts.

In light of all this, it is misguided for those who write pop psychology books to suggest that we should always have high self-esteem. On the days that we are not living up to appropriate expectations, we ought to have lower self-esteem than on those days when we are meeting those expectations. To have high self-esteem when we are "missing the mark" is inappropriate as is having low self-esteem when we are "hitting the mark."

It is not an indication of psychological problems if our self-esteem changes from day to day. Whether we like it or not, as long as we are human our successes and expectations will fluctuate and we will experience the roller-coaster ride of varying degrees of self-esteem.

"Self-worth" is a whole different matter. Our worth as human beings has to do with one thing and one thing only: God created us in His image. The Bible says it pretty clearly: "So God created man in His own image; in the image of God he created him; male and female he created them."[7] Later on in the same chapter of Genesis, it says "God saw everything that He had made, and indeed it was very good."[8]

Your worth never fluctuates because it is always anchored in the fact that the Creator made you and "God doesn't make junk." While your self-esteem goes up and down each day, your worth is stable. You may *feel* absolutely worthless at times and extremely worthwhile at other times, but those feelings don't change the fact that God made you in His image and blessed you with complete worth.

What does it mean to be made in God's image? It means that you have some characteristics in common with God. Six come to mind:

- You are a spiritual being (Numbers 16:22; Hebrews 12:9).
- You think (Isaiah 29:24).
- You have emotions (Deuteronomy 8:5; Psalm 104:15; Romans 9:2).
- You have a conscience (John 8:9; Romans 2:15).
- You have a will (Romans 7:15–25; I Timothy 6:9; James 4:4).
- You long for intimacy (Psalm 63:1; Genesis 2:18).

The good news is that we bear God's image, but the bad news is that all of these characteristics have been tainted by sin. We all struggle in these six areas. We are spiritual beings, but we often lead unspiritual lives because we live according to our fleshly desires. We think, but our thoughts are often irrational and unrealistic. We have emotions, but they are sometimes too strong, too weak, or miss the mark altogether. We have a conscience, but it is often deadened by repetitive sin. We have a will, but it is often trained in the direction of choosing wrong. Finally, we long for intimacy, but we sometimes seek to fulfill this need through relationships or things that aren't capable of satisfying this thirst. With spiritual rebirth, our conscience, thoughts, feelings, and actions all start moving in the right direction again.

Our God-given characteristics distinguish us from sewer rats. A rat has no spirit (in the religious sense of the word), it has no conscience, and it doesn't think, feel, or willfully act on the same level we do (although I would agree that we humans sometimes act no better than rats). Humans are the only beings God created in His image. They are the apex of all that He created on earth. Two further statements from the Bible might help here:

- "You have made him [man] a little lower than the angels, / And You have crowned him with glory and honor. / You have made him to have dominion over the works of Your hands; / You have put all things under his feet."[9]
- "I will praise You, for I am fearfully and wonderfully made; / Marvelous are Your works, / and that my soul knows very well."[10]

I want to stress something here that far too many Christians forget. Becoming a Christian doesn't give you more worth than a non-Christian. Every person on this earth is made in God's image, so everyone is blessed by God with worth.

The good news for you if you are a Christian, though, is that when Christ became Lord of your life, some additional truths kicked in. Try these on for size:

- You were made holy (1 Corinthians 1:2).
- You were set free from the law of sin and death (Romans 8:2).
- You were given access to God (Ephesians 3:12).
- You were brought out of darkness into the light (Ephesians 5:8).
- All of your needs were supplied (Philippians 4:19).
- You were made complete (Colossians 2:10).
- You were forgiven once and for all (Ephesians 1:7).
- You were given an inheritance (Ephesians 1:11).
- You were brought near to God (Ephesians 2:13).

When you become a Christian, you still have the same worth as everyone else, but you have a completely new identity. You go from being Satan's child to God's child. You go from inheriting hell to inheriting heaven. You go from being an enemy of God to being His friend. How's that for a new you?

In the world, you have worth if you are smart, attractive, wealthy, talented, or some combination. In the Bible, you have complete, unchanging worth simply because God made you. You don't have to protect your worth, because it needs no protection; it is an undeniable fact that will never change. Sadly, far too many of us try to find worth through our jobs, looks, income, family, or something else.

One word of caution before I close. Whatever you choose to make your source of personal worth will ultimately become your god. Don't let that fact escape your attention. If you make how you look your source of worth, looks become your god. If you make money your source of worth, money becomes your god. If you make your job your source of worth, work becomes your god.

Choose your god carefully.

CHAPTER 3

Pop psychology myth #3:

YOU CAN'T LOVE OTHERS UNTIL YOU LOVE YOURSELF

The popular singer Whitney Houston had a huge hit sometime back with the song, "The Greatest Love of All." One verse in the song especially stands out to me. It says, "Learning to love yourself is the greatest love of all."

The idea that self-love is the greatest love of all is another myth that is quite common in pop psychology books. This myth is closely associated with another widely held idea: You can't really love others until you love yourself. Both ideas *seem* true enough. Remember, though, some notions that seem right to us often lead to personal ruin. Let me give you some examples of pop psychology books that teach these ideas and then tell you why they are so deadly to our souls.

Remember our friend, Peter McWilliams, the author of *Life 101* and the guy who believes that people are basically good because when you look into a baby's eyes they radiate goodness? Well, not only is he an expert on human nature, he is an expert on love as well. How do we know? Because Mr. McWilliams has written a book on the topic, entitled *Love 101*.

McWilliams tells us in the opening of *Love 101* that he is not "AN IDEAL SPECIMEN OF A SELF-LOVING PERSON" (his emphasis, not mine) but "just a person who has been struggling with the notion of loving myself since 1967." With twenty-eight years under his belt, McWilliams states, "I finally feel as though I have something worth sharing."

It doesn't take McWilliams very long to show us where he is headed in *Love 101*. The subtitle of the book says it all: "To Love Oneself Is the Beginning of a Lifelong Romance." Maybe I am overreacting a bit, but the idea of having a lifelong romance with myself sounds misguided and pathological. (I sure hope it doesn't mean sending myself flowers or love letters.)

McWilliams emphasizes loving yourself as the greatest love of all in the introduction. He writes:

> What if you were about to meet your perfect lover?
> What if you knew this lover better than anyone

else in the world, and this lover knew you better than anyone else?

What if you liked the same food, loved the same movies, listened to the same music, rooted for the same teams, enjoyed the same friends, were fascinated by the same books, had the same spiritual beliefs, cared about the same causes, and shared the same goals?

What if you absolutely knew you two could live together comfortably?

What if this lover always had your best interests at heart?

What if you were brought before a large door and told that, behind the door, was the love of your life?

You straighten your hair, pop a Certs, take a deep breath, open the door . . .

[Turn the page]

. . . and find yourself face-to-face . . .

[Turn the page]

. . . with a mirror.[1]

Personally, I think the first thing I would do is scream! Second, I would be extremely disappointed that my "perfect" lover is me. Third, I would wonder how I and the "love of my life" would ever have kids. Surely, McWilliams is kidding us.

McWilliams is dead serious. He says, "Who else is more qualified to love you than you? Who else knows what you want, precisely when you want it, and is always around to supply it?" I will answer these questions before the chapter is over, but let me suggest that the best answer isn't "Me."

Not only does McWilliams believe that you should be the love of your life, he also believes the other half of the myth. Listen as he enlightens us: "If, on the other hand, you have been gradually coming to the seemingly forbidden conclusion that before we can truly love another, or allow another to properly love us, we must first learn to love ourselves—then this book is for you."[2] There it is: the old "You can't love others until you love yourself" myth. Did you notice that he even adds a new twist—not only can you not love others until you love yourself, but others can't love *you* until you love yourself.

Peter McWilliams is not alone in teaching these ideas. Melody Beattie, author of the mega-best-seller *Codependent No More,* believes the same thing. One of the chapters in her book is entitled, "Have a Love Affair with Yourself" (I knew it. I am going to have to send myself flowers and love letters!) Beattie suggests that "we need to love ourselves and make a commitment to ourselves" and "the love we give and receive will be enhanced by the love we give ourselves."[3]

In her book, *Letting Go of Stress,* Dr. Jackie Schwartz also emphasizes the importance of learning to love yourself. And Dr. Schwartz has found a way for us to give and receive love in one fell swoop. She recommends that you write a love letter and "tell yourself all the attributes you cherish about yourself, the things that really please, comfort, and excite you."[4] She also encourages you to write these letters to "reflect what a wonderful person you are."[5] (There it is in black and white: You are actually supposed to write yourself a love letter. Flowers to yourself are just a phone call away.)

Schwartz tells us about the love letter she wrote to herself. She states "[I] chose the most elegant stationary I could find. I was worth the best."[6] She also explains how she entrusted her love letter to a friend and asked her friend to mail the letter to her at some later time. Getting the letter a couple of months later, she relates how it brightened her day and her week. Schwartz liked the idea so much, she repeated the same process with a different friend in another city. I guess this is one way to make sure you get some mail.

The emphasis on self-love in these and other self-help books reminds me of the story of Narcissus, told by Roman writer Ovid in the *Metamorphoses*. Many people fall in love with Narcissus because he is such a beautiful young man, yet he is filled with pride and rejects their love.

One of those rejected by Narcissus puts a curse on him: "May he fall in love and not have what he loves." This curse is answered by the goddess Nemesis. Narcissus approaches a pool of water that is perfectly still and smooth. Bending down to get a drink of water, he sees what he believes to be someone else's reflection. He reaches down into the water, yet he is unable to grasp what he so desperately desires.

Narcissus is so close to the image but so far from being able to have it as his own. "Has anyone ever had as much longing as I have?" he asks. In the midst of his misery, he suddenly realizes that the image he has fallen in love with is his own. Like the people he rejected, Narcissus suffers because he cannot possess what he has seen in the pool.

Self-love advocates often try to move you in the direction of falling in love with your own image, focusing on what a wonderful person you are and how you need to cherish yourself above all things. All this brings to mind what my daughter Ashley once said to me: "Dad, we need to love ourselves but not fall all over ourselves." Ah, the wisdom of a child!

Now, you might be wondering, "Chris, you seem so against self-love, so what's the alternative? Should we hate ourselves? And how is it possible to love someone else if you don't love yourself?"

The Bible's View of Self-Love and Loving Others

The Bible does *not* teach self-love. Never has and never will. Oh, sure, some people say it does. "Under the influence of humanistic psychologists like Carl

Rogers and Abraham Maslow, many of us Christians have begun to see our need for self-love and self-esteem," Bruce Narramore states in his book, *You're Someone Special.*[7] Interesting, isn't it, that the source of the "influence" is humanistic psychology rather than the Bible.

Walter Trobisch adds his voice to the cry for self-love. In his book, *Love Yourself,* he states, "Self-love is thus the prerequisite and the criterion for our conduct towards our neighbor . . . without self-love there can be no love for others . . . You cannot love God unless you first love yourself."[8] Phillip Captain echoes the same idea in his book, *Eight Stages of Christian Growth.* He says, "Actually, our ability to love God and to love our neighbor is limited by our ability to love ourselves. We cannot love God more than we love our neighbor and we cannot love our neighbor more than we love ourselves."[9]

Does the Bible teach self-love? Does it teach that we can't love others until we love ourselves? Let's allow Christ Himself to answer these questions.

Christ was once asked, "Teacher, which is the greatest commandment in the law?" He answered, "You shall love the LORD your God with all your heart, with all your soul, and with all your mind. This is the first and great commandment. And the second is like it: You shall love your neighbor as yourself."[10] This is one of the most important statements made in all of the Bible, and it bears directly on our discussion.

The word for "love" that is being used in these verses is *agape*. Paul Brownback, in his book, *The Danger of Self-Love,* notes that the word *agape* is used in the Bible to convey a combination of will and action. W. E. Vine, in his *An Expository Dictionary of New Testament Words,* notes, "Christian love, whether exercised toward the brethren, or toward men generally is not an impulse from the feelings, it does not always run with the natural inclinations, nor does it spend itself only upon those for who some affinity is discovered."[11] Agape love is not feeling-based love; it is based on choosing to do what is best for others.

The other word that is translated as "love" in the New Testament is *philia,* which has to do with personal liking and affection. Philadelphia, the city of brotherly love, gets it name from this Greek word. Brownback notes that philia "is not based primarily on calculated analysis of a situation and the people involved, nor is it basically volitional. It is a natural, uncalculated enjoyment of another person."[12] Philia is actually the kind of love that many personal growth authors are talking about when they say we should cherish ourselves and be our own best friend.

Christ is *not* commanding us to *feel* love for God and people; He is commanding us to direct our wills toward action on behalf of God and others. Second, it is clear that Christ is only teaching two commandments here. The first and greatest is to love God, the second is to love your neighbor. There is no third commandment to love yourself, even though people often distort these verses to say just that. These verses are actually telling us to love our neighbor as we *already* love ourselves. The Bible doesn't teach you to love yourself; it is already your natural inclination to do so.

Agape love for ourselves is not something we have to worry about doing because "no one ever hated his own flesh, but nourishes it and cherishes it."[13] The Bible is basically saying that the problem we have in life is not with loving ourselves but with learning to love God and others.

To take this one step further, the Bible actually warns us against the kind of self-love in many pop psychology books. Listen to these words: "But know this, that in the last days perilous times will come: For men will be *lovers of themselves* [emphasis mine], lovers of money, boasters, proud, blasphemers, disobedient to parents, unthankful, unholy, unloving, unforgiving, slanderers, without self-control, brutal, despisers of good, traitors, headstrong, haughty, lovers of pleasure rather than lovers of God, having a form of godliness but denying its power. And from such people turn away!"[14] Sounds descriptive of the world we live in, doesn't it?

The phrase "lovers of themselves" uses the Greek word *philia* (a natural response), not *agape* (a volitional one). The Bible discourages the very kind of love that many self-help authors encourage—having strong affection for yourself, cherishing yourself, being your own best friend, feeling you are wonderful. The "terrible times" coming (if they are not already here) are characterized by the self-love promoted by pop psychology book after pop psychology book.

Now let's tackle the question, Do I have to love myself before I can love others? If we accept the biblical teaching that we already love ourselves, this question now becomes moot. We don't have to ask whether we should love ourselves first; we already do anyway. And, if real love is willfully acting to help someone, we can choose to love others any time we want.

You can feel intense dislike, even hatred, toward yourself or another person and choose to act lovingly. Granted, this is a difficult thing to do, but it is difficult because we human beings have this unfortunate tendency to let our feelings rule our lives. I don't believe in ignoring our feelings, but they need to be secondary to doing what is best for ourselves and others.

Let me show you how all of this might play out in a typical counseling session. Let's say I have a client who struggles with overeating. She has been trying to beat this problem for years with little success. Here is how the biblical teachings on self-love and loving others might come into play.

Suppose I am counseling Cindy, a thirty-five-year-old woman who weighs over 200 pounds, and I ask her the obvious question: "Why do you overeat?"

Cindy looks down at her hands, twists uncomfortably in her chair, and then replies, "I overeat because I hate myself. I've always hated myself. I just need to learn to love myself and then I'll quit overeating."

"I know it seems that way to you, but let me suggest an alternative interpretation. I don't think you really hate yourself. I think you actually love yourself, and your overeating is a misguided way of trying to show it."

"I'm not sure I'm following you."

"Well, when you said you hate yourself, weren't you really saying you *feel* that way toward yourself?"

"Yes, I guess so."

"Well, real love isn't based in feelings. Real love is a willful action to make things better. When you eat, I think you are trying to make things better. Unfortunately, that action is actually hurting you."

"I hadn't thought about it that way before. You mean my overeating is a destructive effort to love myself?"

"Exactly. Think of it another way. If you *really* hated yourself, wouldn't you be glad that you are destroying yourself through overeating? I think the fact that you are so bothered by your overeating indicates that you really do want the best for yourself."

"Yes, it really upsets me when I overeat, which wouldn't be the case if I really did hate myself. So what I need to do is to *really* love myself by acting in a constructive way?"

"Yes. That would mean doing concrete things: joining a diet group, exercising, and shopping smarter at the grocery store, regardless of how you feel each day. It would also mean doing what it takes to face the underlying issues that cause you to become frustrated and overeat. Those would be genuine acts of love toward yourself that would really make a positive difference in your life. Also, I think those steps would help destroy your feelings of self-disgust."

"So instead of waiting until I feel love for myself, I just need to act lovingly toward myself. Then more pleasant feelings will come along as well?"

This counseling scenario is contrived, of course. Usually, it is much harder to get someone to choose to act constructively rather than be controlled by their feelings. When we feel hatred or disgust toward ourselves, we usually are not inclined to do anything to help ourselves out. Yet, the dialogue above captures a very important biblical truth: We naturally love ourselves; we just need to be wise in how we express that love.

While the Bible doesn't teach self-love or self-hate, it does quite frequently teach about the importance of humility, brokenness, and self-denial. Paul Vitz, in his book, *Psychology as Religion: The Cult of Self-Worship,* drives this home:

> The relentless and single-minded search for and glorification of the self is at direct cross purposes

with the Christian injunction to *lose* thyself. Certainly Jesus Christ neither lived nor advocated a life that would qualify by today's standards as "self-actualized." For the Christian the self is the problem, not the potential paradise. Understanding this problem involves an awareness of sin, especially the sin of pride; correcting this condition requires the practice of such un-self-actualized states as contrition and penitence, humility, obedience, and trust in God.[15]

Here, for example, are a sampling of teachings from the Bible that have to do with the importance of humility:

- "He scorns the scornful, but gives grace to the humble."[16]
- "[Walk] with all lowliness and gentleness, with longsuffering."[17]
- "Let nothing be done through selfish ambition or conceit, but in lowliness of mind let each esteem others better than himself."[18]
- "Then Jesus said to His disciples, 'If anyone desires to come after Me, let him deny himself, and take up his cross, and follow Me.'"[19]

When you boil it all down, believing you have to love yourself before you can love others is just a convenient excuse for not doing the hard work of being a loving person. Agape love is often difficult and painful, and many of us run from it for those reasons alone. While we use the excuse "I've got to love myself before I can love others," so many people are starving to death emotionally and spiritually for lack of love.

The Bible provides us with an important passage on the "order" of love:

Beloved, let us love one another, for love is of God; and everyone who loves is born of God and knows God. He who does not love does not know God, for God is love. In this the love of God was manifested toward us, that God has sent His only begotten Son into the world, that we might live through Him. In this is love, not that we loved God, but that He loved us and sent His Son to be the propitiation for our sins. Beloved, if God so loved us, we also ought to love one another. No one has seen God at any time. If we love one another, God abides in us, and His love has been perfected in us.[20]

Notice the order of things presented in this passage. First, God loves us. Second, we receive God's love and are able to love Him back. Third, we then are able to love others. Pop psychology books often have the whole thing backwards. First, love yourself. Second, love others. Third, love God if you happen to believe in him, her, or it. Folks, there is no possible way that you can *properly* love yourself, others, or God without starting with God's love. Without God's love working in our hearts, we will never really love ourselves or anyone else.

More than a few of us have bought into the whole cultural kit and caboodle of believing in man's innate goodness, believing in *self*-worth, and believing we must love ourselves before we can love others. Those three myths form an "unholy trinity," which is destroying so many of us and the world we live in. It is past time to let those three lies go back into the horrible pit of darkness they came from. Man is not basically good, worth comes only from God, and you can (agape) love yourself and others right now regardless of your feelings because God first (agape) loved you.

What do you suppose would have happened if Narcissus had seen God's face in the pool's reflection rather than his own face? The face of perfect love might have completely overwhelmed him if his heart wasn't already hardened into stone. God's love is unconditional and will never fail you. It is out to do you good, not harm. It disciplines you when you are off base because it doesn't want you destroying yourself or others. It is a love that pursues you every moment of every day but respects the fact that you are free to reject it. It is a love that will carry you through the toughest things life can throw at you and a love that yearns to gather you in its arms when you are hurting the most deeply. It is a love that will not rest until it has brought you safely home.

Whitney Houston was wrong. The greatest love of all is not the love we have for ourselves. The greatest love of all is the love God has for us. Nothing surpasses it. And when Peter McWilliams asks, "Who else is more qualified to love you than you? Who else knows what you want, precisely what you want, and is always around to provide it?" the real answer to that question is "God."

CHAPTER 4

Pop psychology myth #4:

YOU SHOULDN'T JUDGE ANYONE

I'm sure that at one time or another, we have all heard statements like the following ones:

- "You're just being judgmental!"
- "You shouldn't criticize yourself!"
- "Who are you to judge me?"

We've probably even said them ourselves. In our culture, we often hear that it is wrong to judge others, and I wonder if that doesn't come, in part, from reading pop psychology books.

Remember McKay and Fanning, authors of the popular book *Self-Esteem*? They believe that making moral judgments about people is a serious no-no and that we must stop as soon as possible—like yesterday. "Hard as it sounds, you must give up moral opinions about the actions of others," McKay and Fanning say. "Cultivate instead the attitude that they have made the best choice available, given their awareness and needs at the time. Be clear that while their behavior may not feel or be good for you, it is not bad."[1] They also suggest that you abstain from "evaluating as good or bad or right or wrong things you read, see on TV, or observe on the street. This includes assaults, terrorists bombings, political corruptions, and so on."[2]

There's more to this depraved way of thinking:

> What does it mean that people choose the highest good? It means that you are doing the best you can at any given time. It means that people always act according to their prevailing awareness, needs, and values. Even the terrorist planting bombs to hurt the innocent is making a decision based on his or her highest good. It means you cannot blame people for what they do. Nor can you blame yourself. No matter how distorted or mistaken a person's awareness is, he or she is innocent and blameless. That's because no one can act differently than his or her current awareness permits, and you can change only when your awareness changes.[3]

I guess people who sell illegal drugs are off the hook because "you cannot blame people for what they do." I guess people who abuse children are off the hook because "no one can act differently than his or her current awareness permits." I guess people who murder are off the hook because they "choose the highest good" and "are doing the best [they] can at any given time." Hey, you are just being judgmental if you think otherwise!

This was especially tough advice to hear in 1995 when a car bomb exploded in front of the Alfred P. Murrah building in Oklahoma City, killing 169 innocent men, women, and children. Yet, according to McKay and Fanning, we shouldn't judge the people who did this because "even the terrorist planting bombs to hurt the innocent is making a decision based on his or her highest good." This is how sickening some of the advice from pop psychology can be.

McKay and Fanning make a very interesting assumption when they teach "You are doing the best you can at any given time." Is that really true? Do you always do the best you are capable of as a worker? As a spouse? A parent? A friend? A tennis player? A whatever? I think if you are honest with yourself, the answer is "no." None of us can truthfully say we always do our best, and it is nonsense to suggest that we do.

Put Adolf Hitler's name into this discussion, and I think you will see what I mean. He represents the very picture of human evil. I would argue that Hitler's heart was naturally "hard" at birth (remember, he was "born in Adam" and had a sinful nature at birth), became even harder along the way because of repetitive immoral choices, and ultimately became so hardened that he was enslaved to doing evil.

Now, do we buy into McKay and Fanning's belief that Hitler did the best he could and, therefore, we must not judge or blame him? Even if Hitler was doing "the best he could given his awareness at the time," how does that make what he did less evil and him less responsible?

McKay and Fanning suggest that we "must give up moral opinions about the actions of others." This is incredibly misguided and dangerous. If someone broke into McKay or Fanning's home, stole everything of value, raped and murdered the family, and burned the home to the ground to hide the evidence, do you think either one wouldn't make some moral judgments? Do you think they would refrain from making moral judgments if they had had loved ones killed in the Oklahoma City bombing?

When McKay and Fanning teach how bad it is to make moral judgments, they are actually making a moral judgment: Making moral judgements is bad. And they make moral judgments throughout their book. For example, in an earlier quote, they said, "No matter how distorted or mistaken a person's awareness is . . ." Isn't that judging? Isn't that saying that there are less distorted, less mistaken levels of awareness?

And, if there are, who is going to judge what constitutes "good" awareness versus "bad" awareness?

There is something quite troubling about teaching people the idea that they always do their best and that to judge anyone's actions is wrong. How many parents, for example, have used the line with their kids (young or grown-up) when challenged about their parenting, "Well, dear, I did the best I could"? That makes it all too easy to avoid facing the possibility that they didn't do their best, not for the purpose of condemning themselves but for the purpose of honestly examining what they did, making amends, and making needed changes in who they are now. When we don't give something our complete effort, to say "I did the best I could" is a cop-out.

Before I go into the biblical view on making moral judgments, I want to give you a short "pop quiz." Following are brief descriptions of real stories taken directly from the newspaper over the last year or so. Read each and see if you can bring yourself to agree with McKay and Fanning's statement, "It is wrong to judge the individual(s) involved because they were doing the best they could."

_____ A man grabs a mother's purse in the parking lot of a shopping mall, causing her to drop her baby. In fleeing the scene, the man runs over the baby with his car.

_____ Two teenagers go on a shopping spree with their grandmother's life savings—$26,500. They spend all but $8,100 of the money on a trip to Walt Disney World.

_____ A woman kills her seven-month-old nephew with an electric stun gun in an effort to quiet him down.

_____ The former president of the United Way steals nearly $600,000 from the charity, and lavishes some of it on teenage girls in an effort to seduce them.

_____ A student inflates his grade point average, forges school transcripts, and provides letters of recommendation from people who don't exist in his application to attend Yale University. He is accepted into the university.

_____ The boyfriend of the mother of a four-year-old girl punishes the little girl for cursing at him by wrapping her in a comforter and stuffing her under a waterbed as punishment. The little girl dies of asphyxiation.

_____ Two juveniles, ages ten and eleven, drop a five-year-old boy to his death from the fourteenth-floor window of an abandoned apartment building because the child wouldn't steal candy for them.

It is complete foolishness to teach that people always do the best they can, and, because they do, we must stop making moral judgments. Doing so would make the world a crazier place than it already is.

Now let's turn to what the Bible has to say about judging yourself and others.

· · · · · · · · · · · ·

The Bible's View of Judging

The Bible actually teaches us to judge ourselves and others! But let me explain the kind of judgments the Bible teaches us to make.

First, the standard for judging our own behavior or the behavior of others is the Bible itself. Unfortunately, popular opinion or personal feelings are often used as the standard for right and wrong in this country, meaning that right and wrong can (and often does) change over time. For example, it used to be wrong to engage in premarital sex. It used to be wrong to have children out of wedlock. It used to be wrong to live together without being married. Now, all of these things are accepted by a fair number of people in our culture.

The Bible is the ultimate standard of right and wrong, not anything else. What it says goes, for now and forevermore. So if the Bible says murder is wrong, murder is wrong. If the Bible says stealing is wrong, stealing is wrong. If the Bible said eating popcorn was wrong (it doesn't, thank goodness), then eating popcorn would be wrong.

Now that we have that established, a second critical issue needs to be examined. Given that we have a standard for right and wrong called the Bible, how are we to judge ourselves and others?

Very humbly.

The passages in Matthew and Luke that contain the statement, "Judge not, that you be not judged,"[4] are teaching against self-righteous, unjust, and hypocritical judging. The real point of these passages is, "You hypocrite, first take the plank out of your own eye, and then you will see to remove the speck from your brother's eye." The thrust of all this is that we are going to make judgments about moral and immoral behavior, but we need to do so through the lens of Scripture and after having looked honestly at our own actions first.

What a horribly difficult thing to do. I don't know about you, but I find myself launching into judgmental thoughts about people far too often without stopping to look at myself first. I am a hypocrite in doing so. So are you when you do the same thing.

When a terrorist blows up an airplane and kills hundreds of innocent people, that is murder and that is wrong. Judging it so is not wrong. What I have to watch out for is my own tendency to make that judgment as if I have never done anything wrong—or will never do something that evil.

Christ judged people's actions all the time, yet He never sinned. He offered moral opinions everywhere He went. Yet Christ said, "I can of Myself do nothing.

As I hear, I judge; and My judgment is righteous, because I do not seek My own will but the will of the Father who sent Me."[5] What is different about Christ is that He lived in a completely nonhypocritical way. He did everything He told people to do, and He didn't do the things He told people not to do. Christ perfectly practiced what He preached. No one else who has walked this planet can say that. Not me, not you (sorry for judging).

The Bible has more to say on the subject of judging: "You shall do no injustice in judgment. You shall not be partial to the poor, nor honor the person of the mighty. In righteousness you shall judge your neighbor."[6] "Open your mouth, judge righteously, / And plead the cause of the poor and needy."[7]

Moral judgments need to be made by all of us about our own behavior and the behavior of others. The real problem isn't that we judge, but that we do so blindly and arrogantly.

So judge whomever you will—but only if you are using God's standards and have examined your own sins first. Then the moral judgments you make will be appropriate and helpful.

CHAPTER 5

Pop psychology myth #5:

ALL GUILT IS BAD

I lied recently. I don't like to admit it, but I did. It was during a trip to Philadelphia to do a seminar. I landed at the airport and headed toward the baggage claim area. On the way to pick up my bags, I passed a bank of telephones that provided direct lines to the various hotels nearby. The Marriott was on the list, so I picked up the phone and dialed it.

"This is Chris Thurman. I'm staying at your hotel tonight, and I just arrived at the airport. Would you mind sending your courtesy van to come pick me up?"

"Not at all, Mr. Thurman. Have you picked up your bags yet?"

Having traveled quite a bit over the past ten years doing seminars, I have had conversations like this with numerous hotels before. Up to that point, when asked if I had my bags I had told the truth and answered "No." The hotel would then tell me to call them back when I had my bags, and they would send the courtesy van then. That would usually tack on another fifteen or twenty minutes—sometimes even more—before I was picked up. So, being the impatient, Type A person that I am, I answered, "Yes, I have them."

I hustled over to the baggage claim area, hoping that my bags would come quickly so that I would be ready to go when the courtesy van arrived. I waited. And waited. And waited. Sure enough, the Marriott courtesy van pulled up outside looking for me, and my bags were nowhere in sight. The driver waited a few minutes, then drove off. Finally, my bags came, so I went back over to the phones to call the hotel again.

I tell you all this not only to own up to the fact that I sometimes lie but to raise an issue that pop psychology books sometimes mutilate: justifiable guilt. Read certain books, and you begin to wonder if guilt is something we are supposed to experience at all. In some of these books, guilt is actually viewed as something that should be completely eliminated from our lives. Let me give you a small sampling.

In his best-seller, *Your Erroneous Zones,* Dr. Wayne Dyer, the author of a number of best-sellers on personal growth, has a chapter entitled, "The Useless Emotions—Guilt and Worry." First, let me say I agree with him that worry is useless. As Mickey Rivers, a former major league baseball player, was reported to have said, "If I can do something about a problem, why worry about it? If I can't do anything about a problem, why worry about it?" I think that's a pretty good philosophy. But, throw guilt into the category of "useless," and you have made a fundamental mistake.

Dr. Dyer calls guilt "the most useless of all erroneous zone behaviors"; it keeps you "immobilized as a result of past behavior."[1] He believes guilt originates from two sources: childhood memories and current misbehavior. Dyer says, "Thus you can look at all of your guilt either as reactions to leftover imposed standards in which you are still trying to please an absent authority figure, or as the result of trying to live up to self-imposed standards which you really don't buy, but for some reason pay lip service to. In either case, it is stupid, and, more important, useless behavior."[2]

Dyer goes on to say that "guilt is not a natural behavior" and that our "guilt zones" must be "exterminated, spray-cleaned and sterilized forever." One way to exterminate your "guilt zones," according to Dr. Dyer, is to "do something you know is bound to result in feelings of guilt." For example, he suggests you "take a week to be alone if you've always wanted to do so, despite the guilt-engendering protestations from other members of your family. . . . These kinds of behaviors will help you tackle that omnipresent guilt that so many sectors of the environment are adept at helping you to choose."[3]

Dyer mentions how he counseled one client who was having an extramarital affair. He said this man's guilt over the affair "did not improve his marriage" and—get this—"even prevented him from enjoying his affair." According to Dyer, his client had two choices: "He could recognize that he was devoting his present to feeling guilty because it was easier than examining his marriage closely and going to work on it," or "he could learn to accept his behavior."[4]

Let's stop and take a look at that advice. This client, according to the advice of this best-selling author, needs to do whatever it takes to stop feeling guilty, even if it means accepting "that he [the client] condoned extramarital sexual exploration" and "that his value system encompassed behavior which many people condemn."[5]

Is it possible that Dr. Dyer's client is feeling guilty because he is, in fact, doing something wrong? (There I go being judgmental again!) And is it possible that he is going to keep experiencing guilt until he stops doing wrong or his conscience hardens? Is it also possible that getting people to accept their wrong behavior as who they are doesn't really address their guilt? Instead of examining the moral implications of the man's actions, Dyer just wants the guy to do whatever it takes to stop feeling guilty even if that means learning to enjoy adultery. (Oops! I mean "extramarital sexual exploration." Don't you just love the way these people use words?)

Dyer closes his section on guilt by calling it "a convenient tool for manipulation" and "a futile waste of time."[6] Guilt can definitely be used to manipulate people, and there is a type of guilt that is, in fact, "a futile waste of time." But Dyer doesn't seem to think that there is a version of guilt that is good.

Remember how McKay and Fanning suggested that we need to quit making moral judgments about ourselves and others? Underneath their "expert" advice is the same basic myth: People should not feel guilty because they are doing the best they can, given their current awareness. Even if you commit the most heinous crime, guilt is inappropriate. What an incredible rationalization for doing whatever you want to do and not caring about who it affects or how it affects them!

One final "authority" on guilt needs to be heard before we see what the Bible has to say about the topic: Ann Landers. I have enjoyed reading Landers's column throughout the years, often agreeing with the advice she dispenses. But, on the issue of guilt, she is a tad off base. She, like Dyer and McKay and Fanning, believes guilt is a bad deal:

> One of the most painful, self-mutilating, time-and energy-consuming exercises in the human experience is guilt . . . It can ruin your day—or your week or your life—if you let it. It turns up like a bad penny when you do something dishonest, hurtful, tacky, selfish, or rotten. . . . Never mind that it was the result of ignorance, stupidity, laziness, thoughtlessness, weak flesh, or clay feet. You did wrong and the guilt is killing you. Too bad. But be assured, the agony you feel is normal . . . Remember guilt is a pollutant and we don't need any more of it in the world.[7]

Really? What happens when people *don't* experience guilt when they do wrong? Aren't they what we refer to as sociopaths? Doesn't the absence of guilt allow many people to do horribly evil things without thinking twice about it?

Compare what Dyer, McKay and Fanning, and Landers teach to the author of a letter that appeared in the April 15, 1985, issue of *U.S. News and World Report:*

> I am the boy who killed his mother. I need to write for two reasons: One, as part of this "culture" I feel I can relate; and, two, to set the record straight about my case.
>
> I disagree with people who say that parents are

to blame. It was not my mom's fault that I was the way I was, and it certainly wasn't her fault that I murdered her. The article says that mother "ignored me until the pressure blew me up." This was the impression I gave to people involved in my case. It is not true. I received no unfair treatment, nor did I have to go through anything that other kids don't go through as a part of growing up. Kids have gone through it for centuries.

The real problem was how I chose to deal with what did happen. I am not saying that things don't happen to cause kids to do things. In my situation, I am the only one to be blamed for what I did and for the immense pain I caused many people. I really need to make that clear. I lied in the beginning due to my own selfishness. I lied so that I would not have to honestly look at who I was and what I had done.

If this is the kind of guilt that certain experts think we ought to eliminate from the world, God help us all. If this is the kind of guilt that can "ruin your day," then all of us need to have our days ruined more often. Too bad Erik and Lyle Menendez didn't have this young man's attitude. Instead, they not only matched evil with evil but blamed it all on Mom and Dad.

The myth "All guilt is bad" is pretty dangerous stuff, I believe, yet far too many people have actually bought into it.

What does the Bible have to say about all of this?

The Bible and Guilt

The Bible teaches that one form of guilt doesn't do anyone any good and another form of guilt is quite appropriate. Let's take a look at both.

The Bible says, "*Godly sorrow* produces repentance leading to salvation, not to be regretted; but the *sorrow of the world* produces death."[8] Notice the critical distinction? The kind of guilt that is "worldly" does not lead to true change in a person's life, whereas "godly sorrow" does. So what is "worldly" sorrow, and what is "godly" sorrow?

To answer that question, allow me to borrow from the book, *Freedom from Guilt* by Bruce Narramore and Bill Counts. The authors believe that these two kinds of reactions to doing something wrong differ in a number of significant ways. Let's take a look at five of them.

First, worldly sorrow (sometimes called "false guilt") causes us to focus on ourselves, whereas godly sorrow (sometimes referred to as "true guilt") leads us to focus on the person or people we have offended. So, if I am late for a meeting with someone, worldly sorrow causes me to focus on how bad I feel about being late, whereas godly sorrow causes me to focus on how my acquaintance feels as he waits for me. Worldly sorrow is self-absorbed; godly sorrow aims to get inside the shoes of the other person.

Second, worldly sorrow causes us to focus on what we have done in the past, whereas godly sorrow causes us to focus on what we can do in the present to correct what we've done. If I cheated on my taxes to save money ten years ago (I didn't, just in case you were wondering), worldly sorrow would keep me focused on that sin. Godly sorrow would prompt me to take corrective action right now: Pay Uncle Sam what I owe and the penalties that go with it. Worldly sorrow, then, focuses on past history, whereas godly sorrow is aimed at the "here and now."

Third, corrective actions that come out of worldly sorrow are motivated by the desire to stop feeling bad. Actions that come out of godly sorrow are motivated by the desire to help the offended person, please God, and promote personal growth. If, for example, I say something unkind to a person, worldly sorrow pushes me to apologize so that I will stop feeling bad. Godly sorrow, on the other hand, prompts me to apologize for the benefit of the person I have hurt. God is pleased because I have just helped one of His "children" and because I did something that helps me to become more mature.

Fourth, worldly sorrow is undergirded by feelings of self-hate and self-disgust, whereas godly sorrow is based on appropriate love, respect, and concern for ourselves. Let's say you have a problem controlling your temper with your kids. Worldly sorrow causes you to hate and condemn yourself when you lose your temper, whereas godly sorrow makes you care enough about yourself to want to change.

Finally, the results of worldly and godly sorrow differ. Worldly sorrow often results in temporary change—but rebellion later on. Godly sorrow results in true change. Why does worldly sorrow result in temporary change and godly sorrow result in lasting change? When you use self-condemnation and self-hatred to try to make yourself change, resentment and bitterness grow in your soul. The resentment and bitterness lead to internal rebellion (you sabotage yourself) because you don't like the method being used to change you.

Let me make this a little clearer, if I can. Think about how this rebellion "dynamic" shows up in relationships between people. You can use condemnation and hatred to motivate your kids to pick up their room by yelling and screaming at them, but chances are they'll get you back later on. Same thing in marriage. You can use hatred and condemnation to pressure your spouse into spending less, helping more around the house, and so on, but watch out. Nobody likes to be treated like that, and your spouse will most likely make you pay sooner or later.

Pop psychology books are correct in discouraging guilt if they are talking about worldly sorrow. That kind of guilt isn't helpful to anyone. It does not mature you, it does not help make someone else's life better, and it does not please God. Satan is out to "kill, steal, and destroy," and worldly sorrow is one of his main weapons. This kind of sorrow puts people in emotional and spiritual bondage.

My own life has been caught up in worldly guilt more often than godly sorrow. I have done and still do rotten things, but I often find myself moving pretty quickly in the direction of focusing on how bad I feel (self-focused) about what I have done (the past). I find myself wanting to change so I can stop feeling bad (wrong motivation). Underneath it all are feelings of self-disgust and self-contempt (wrong attitude toward myself). While I might change for an hour or two, or a day or two, or even a month or two, the old behavior always comes back (rebellion).

There have been those times, though, when I got out of God's way and allowed Him to work through my heart to move me in a much different direction. At those moments, my reaction to personal sin shifts from focusing on me to focusing on the person my actions hurt, from what I did in the past to what I can do right now, from wanting to stop feeling bad to wanting to help someone else feel better, and from condemning myself to appropriately loving myself. Those moments of godly sorrow are truly life changing. The ending of my Philadelphia airport story will show you what I'm talking about.

My normal way of handling the fact that I lied would have been to feel bad about it but make no effort to "repent" when the driver came the second time. I would have continued to feel guilty about what I had done long after it was over, heaped more condemnation on myself, and stayed enslaved to worldly sorrow. God helped me to do otherwise. While I waited for the driver to come back, God gently reminded me that "all fall short of the glory of God" and that He "gives grace to the humble." He helped me to remember how important it is to "confess your sins to one another" in order to be mature and healthy in life. God tenderly nudged me in the direction of doing what was right even though I didn't feel like it.

So, I did. I told the driver what I had done, that I had lied to the people at the hotel about already having my bags when they sent him out the first time. He was amazed by my confession. "During my two years of picking up people at the airport *no one* has ever said it was his fault that they missed the van."

As painful as my confession was, it freed me from the bondage of feeling guilty. It freed me to live life more fully in the present because the past wasn't going to be allowed to be a ball and chain weighing me down.

Godly sorrow, when we experience it, is something we cannot take credit for. It is, after all, *godly* sorrow. It comes from God, or we don't experience it at all. It requires that we quit trying to use our own resources and rely on God's. This whole idea of going to God in order to experience constructive sorrow is a tough thing. I don't know about you, but I want to have godly sorrow over my sins, yet take credit for it as my own creation.

The Bible doesn't teach us to walk around feeling guilty in the self-destructive way that many self-help authors decry. These authors are to be commended for fighting against that kind of guilt, because it does destroy people. But some of these authors go too far in wanting to eliminate guilt altogether. They encourage us in a direction where morals become relative, and nothing is called sin. When something pains our conscience, we simply "accept that our value system encompasses" behavior that God condemns. Nifty mental tricks, if they worked.

Godly sorrow is not "stupid," "a convenient tool for manipulation," "a futile waste of time," "self-mutilating," or a "pollutant." It does not need to be "exterminated, spray-cleaned, and sterilized forever." It is a *gift* from God that helps keep all of us from destroying ourselves and those around us. Can you imagine the world without it?

Is there a type of guilt that actually benefits your life that you would be wise to experience? Are there certain sins in your life that you keep repeating because you keep reacting to them with worldly sorrow? Do you ever turn to God to help you experience the kind of sorrow that can truly turn you around?

These are tough questions. It will take a great deal of courage on your part to answer them honestly. Yet, if you don't answer them, you stand a pretty good chance of experiencing worldly guilt. This kind of guilt makes you miserable every day and increases the chances that you will sin again in the very same way.

Let me challenge you to think about an area of your life that you feel extremely guilty about and to make a commitment to respond to it with godly sorrow. That will mean getting down on your knees and asking God to work through you. Then, it will mean spending some time thinking about how the other person felt. Finally, it will mean doing something now to make amends and help the person you have hurt. The foundation underneath this whole effort is God's love for you, your love for God, and your appropriate love for yourself.

Ask God to help you do this, and see if the results aren't what you wanted all along.

CHAPTER 6

Pop psychology myth #6:

YOU NEED TO THINK POSITIVELY

Dick loves to gamble. Each year he takes several trips to Las Vegas to indulge his urges. Before he leaves on these trips, Dick often talks about how he is going to "break the bank" and come back "filthy rich." Yet, trip after trip, Dick returns with a frown on his face and umpteen excuses for why he lost, rather than won, money. These gambling losses don't keep him from going back to Las Vegas over and over. Deep in his heart, Dick just knows that his day will come; vast wealth will be his.

Dick is what you might call a positive thinker. When he thinks about gambling, it doesn't even enter his mind that he might lose. To Dick, thinking that he might lose money is being negative and defeatist. Sure, he sees more people losing money than winning money during his many trips, and his own experiences in Las Vegas have been similar. But Dick has confidence in himself and only lets his mind dwell on thoughts about coming out on top.

By the way, Dick is more than forty thousand dollars in debt because of his gambling. His wife left him six months ago, he is in danger of losing his job, and the bank foreclosed on his home because he couldn't make his mortgage payments.

I tell you this story because it flies in the face of another myth that is taught in some pop psychology books: "You need to think positively." Book after book on the self-help bookshelves talk about how important it is to fill your mind only with upbeat, pleasant, encouraging thoughts. They say that nothing negative should be allowed to enter your mind; success and happiness are yours if you will just learn to think positively.

Perhaps the most well-known book on the importance of positive thinking is Norman Vincent Peale's classic, *The Power of Positive Thinking*. The book's cover proclaims, "OVER 5 MILLION COPIES IN PRINT," and calls the work "The Greatest Inspirational Best-seller Of Our Time." More than five million copies in print! If any of my books had sold five million copies, I would be in the Caribbean right now on my private yacht. "The Greatest Inspirational Best-seller Of Our

Time!" What a thing to say about a book! I thought the Bible was the greatest inspirational best-seller of our time.

Let me begin by saying that there are many things to recommend about *The Power of Positive Thinking*. Of the gazillion (that's the number between a bazillion and a kazillion) books I read in preparing to write this book, *The Power of Positive Thinking* said more solid things than most. Dr. Peale rightly emphasizes the important influence that our thoughts have on us, pushes the reader to see difficult circumstances as a challenge rather than a threat, and calls all of us to "renew our minds."[1] He talks about God as someone who earnestly wants to help us, encourages prayer as a critical activity in facing our problems, and prods people to live victoriously rather than in defeat. Underneath his words, there appears to be a genuine love for people and a deep-seated desire to help them live a fulfilling life.

You can see why I am a little hesitant to criticize *The Power of Positive Thinking*. It has helped a lot of people live better lives. But allow me to zero in on a few concerns. Peale says that a "more positive pattern of ideas must be given the mind" than those that have to do with our inadequacy and insecurity.[2] Peale believes that "it is important to eliminate from conversations all negative ideas, for they tend to produce tension and annoyance inwardly"[3] and that "whenever a negative thought concerning your personal powers comes to mind, deliberately voice a positive thought to cancel it out."[4] According to Peale, we need to develop a "happiness habit" by "simply practicing happy thinking."[5] He goes on to suggest that "if an unhappiness thought should enter your mind, immediately stop, consciously eject it, and substitute a happiness thought."[6]

Now, you might wonder why some of this bothers me. Two things greatly concern me about what Peale and others in the positive-thinking movement teach. First, the focus is on *positive* thinking, when *realistic* thinking actually needs to be our focus. Second, the focus is on being *happy* when sometimes being *unhappy* is actually more appropriate at the moment. As strange as it may sound, I believe it misguided to encourage people to always think positively and to focus on being happy. Allow me to explain.

Thinking positively when something is actually negative is inappropriate and destructive to our emotional and spiritual health. There are negative things in life, and it is not unhealthy to see them that way. The same principle applies to happiness. Being unhappy at times is actually an indication that you are seeing reality for what it is. Let me give you a couple of examples of why only thinking positive thoughts and only focusing on being happy would actually prevent you from reacting to life in a healthy way.

A number of years ago I counseled a woman whose father died of cancer. My client's father did not believe in God and often made fun of those who did. If the Bible is telling the truth, this man is currently residing in hell and is going to spend eternity there. Should my client try to think positively about that and try to put a happy face on it? Is she falling into negative thinking to see her father's rejection of God as a tragedy? I think not, and I believe my client is healthier in her thinking if she sees her father's death as sad and feels grieved over it.

Certain things in life, no matter what good may ultimately come out of them, are negative and need to be seen that way. To put a positive twist on everything is to create a world that doesn't really exist. Human beings starve to death every day. Human beings murder each other. Human beings mistreat each other. I agree that these realities should not become our sole focus, but Norman Vincent Peale seems to want us either to ignore them or to have some kind of artificially positive attitude toward them. We need to rejoice over the happy things and weep over the sad things—not think positively all the time and develop "a happiness habit."

Let me give you another example. I was flying home from a seminar last week and was reading an article in a magazine about how many people in third-world countries are dying from disease. The article had a picture in it that I will never, ever forget. It showed a man standing in a morgue next to numerous bodies of small children who had died from various diseases, literally stacked on top of each other. The picture was heartbreaking.

Yet, I needed to be bothered by it. It was a necessary reminder to me that life is pretty awful for some people and that my life is so blessed. It shook me out of my narrow, self-pitying way of thinking. There are horribly negative realities in the world that should make all of us weep. *Dwelling* on realities like these doesn't do any good, but not thinking about them because they are negative or attempting to turn them into some kind of positive constricts our worldview and turns us into insensitive people.

Since Peale wrote *The Power of Positive Thinking,* many imitators have come along. Shad Helmstetter, Ph.D., has written a number of very popular books on the power of your "self-talk," the thoughts you have in your mind about situations you encounter in life. In 1982, Dr. Helmstetter wrote a book entitled, *What to Say When You Talk to Your Self.* The front cover of that book reads, "Powerful New Techniques to Program Your Potential for Success!"

First, there aren't any "powerful *new* techniques" in the book. All Dr. Helmstetter does is regurgitate the same old positive-thinking principles and pop psychology notions that have been written about hundreds of times before. Second, isn't it interesting that the book is focused on programming "*your* potential for success." I think I will keel over dead if I ever see a book title or subtitle that says, "Become a Servant and Help Others Become More Successful."

Dr. Helmstetter agrees with Dr. Peale that your thoughts each day dictate your life to you. He even draws on the teachings of the Bible to validate his approach: "As a man thinketh, so is he."[7] Yet, Helmstetter's self-talk principles of positive and negative thought are anything but biblical—or rational.

Let's take a look at what Helmstetter calls "negative" self-talk:

"I just don't have the talent."[8] You know, sometimes the truth of the matter is that a person doesn't have the talent for certain things. I sing a great deal in my car when driving alone (my wife and kids appreciate that), but I don't have the talent to be a great singer. That isn't being negative, that's being honest. Should I tell myself, "Chris, you have the most awesome talent for singing. You could be the next . . ." That would be positive, but also untrue.

On the other hand, if I actually do have the talent to be a great singer and tell myself, "I just don't have the talent," I am being negative and defeatist. Acknowledging talent is fine, even appropriate, and we are only exhibiting false humility if we deny the talent we have been given.

"I just get sick thinking about it."[9] Aren't there certain things in life worth getting "sick" (upset, bothered, hurt) over when we think about them? I get "sick" when I think about that picture I mentioned

earlier of those innocent babies in that morgue. I get "sick" when I think about world hunger. I get "sick" when I think about the homeless. I hope things like that always make me sick. Not to be sickened by the thought of these things means one is no longer human.

"I'm really out of shape."[10] For some people, that is an accurate statement. They are out of shape, and they are not being negative to tell it like it is. Should a guy who is seventy-five pounds overweight and who can't walk up a flight of stairs without difficulty tell himself, "I'm in fantastic shape"? That is certainly positive, but it would be a lie.

"I never have any money left over at the end of the month."[11] I don't, how about you? By the end of the month, my wallet is empty except for charge slips. Again, the truth of the matter is that many people *don't* have any money left over at the end of the month. Should we tell ourselves we are filthy rich at the end of the month and spend money as if that were true?

"I hate my job."[12] Some people do, in fact, hate their jobs! Why is it negative to say so? Saying this doesn't mean there isn't anything about it that you like. The truth of the matter is that some people are currently in jobs that they are not suited for, in jobs in which the conditions are horrible, or both. Hate is a strong word, I admit, but sometimes people feel that negatively and strongly about their jobs. That strong

feeling may prompt them either to do something to make the job better or to look for something else that better suits their gifts and abilities.

According to Helmstetter, all of the statements above are examples of negative self-talk and should be avoided at all costs. To me, while they *could* be examples of negative, self-destructive thinking, they could also be examples of self-talk that is accurate and honest and appropriate for a person to think.

Let's turn from what Helmstetter calls negative self-talk to examples of positive self-talk that he thinks you should tell yourself day by day.

Helmstetter suggests you let the following statements run through your mind as often as possible to help "Program Your Potential for Success!" He believes that it isn't important if what you tell yourself is true or not; if you want it to be true, that's enough. "Because the subconscious mind does not know what is true and what is not, in time it will accept what you are telling it and act on it," he asserts.[13] The idea is that you need to feed yourself carefully worded statements that you want to be true, and your subconscious mind will make them happen.

"You were born with everything you need to live your life in a most exceptional and worthwhile way."[14] Not really. You and I were born with finite intellect, skills, and abilities, and this *fact* interferes with our ability to live life "in a most exceptional and worthwhile way."

All this isn't to say that people don't live what *appear* to be "exceptional and worthwhile" lives, but what *eternal* significance do those lives have? For example, King Solomon was the most "successful" person of his day, and he called all his accomplishments a "meaningless chasing after the wind" and "vanity of vanities" because they were done apart from God. Solomon was smarter than Einstein, wealthier than H. Ross Perot, and more desirable than Brad Pitt, so he wasn't some envious, bitter failure who had been outdone by others. He outdid everyone and then came to his senses—being "exceptional" in the world's eyes is meaningless and empty if God is not the center of it.

The Bible is pretty clear that anything done apart from God is "wood, hay, and stubble" and is going to count for nothing when all is said and done. Without God, none of us possess what it takes to have a *truly* "exceptional and worthwhile" life that will have eternal significance.

"I like how I feel and I like how I think and I like how I do things. I approve of me and I approve of who I am."[15] No matter how much progress you make in life in terms of personal growth, you will still feel, think, and do things that you won't like at times. Saying otherwise doesn't make it so.

And what does it mean to say, "I approve of me and I approve of who I am"? There are things about me that I *don't* approve of, how about you? Is that a sign of mental illness or mental health? If Helmstetter is suggesting that we love ourselves (agape style) no matter how we act, okay. Agape love is a commitment to willfully and actively "Love the sinner, hate the sin." What Helmstetter is talking about sounds to me like a commitment to "Love the sinner, accept the sin." He appears to be suggesting complete self-acceptance no matter how we act.

"I am positive. I am confident. I radiate good things. If you look closely, you can even see a glow around me."[16] You have been too close to a radioactive waste site if you can see a glow around yourself. This is just more positive-thinking mumbo jumbo that turns you into some kind of alien from outer space.

Let's take a look at what the Bible has to say about how your thinking impacts your life.

. . . .
The Bible and Your Thoughts

Norman Vincent Peale and Shad Helmstetter are both correct when they draw on the biblical principle, "As he thinks in his heart, so is he."[17] Our thoughts play a critical role in determining our emotions and actions each day. The Bible does in fact teach that your life will reflect what you believe. Yet Peale and Helmstetter don't tell you the whole story about where the Bible stands on this issue. Allow me to try.

The Bible does not teach positive thinking or negative thinking. What the Bible does teach, first and foremost, is *truthful thinking*. Sometimes, the truth is positive and will lead to pleasant emotions. For example, God unconditionally loves you. That is true, it is positive, and thinking about it leads to joy. Sometimes, though, the truth is "negative," and thinking about it will lead to painful emotions. The Bible teaches, for example, that the wicked sometimes get what the righteous deserve.[18] That is true, it is negative, and thinking about it is discouraging.

The emphasis in the Bible is not on positive or negative thinking but on "developing the mind of Christ." This is complete truth. Everything Christ thought was true, so all his emotions and actions were "on the mark." Yet, remember, Christ was once called a "man familiar with sorrow," and he had strong, painful reactions to life in many instances. He wept when Lazarus died, he got angry with the moneylenders in the temple, and he sweat blood in the Garden of Gethsemane because he was so grieved about his upcoming death on the cross. Having the mind of Christ doesn't mean you will always be happy, but it does mean that you will see things for what they really are and react appropriately.

The Bible teaches that God's thoughts are far superior to ours and that He is the source of all truth. His thoughts need to become our own if we are going to end up with the right "tapes" in our minds. Read a book like Shad Helmstetter's and you get the distinct impression that he wants to quote from the Bible but not allow the Bible or the God who wrote it to be the ultimate authority.

In the self-talk world of Helmstetter, humans get to play God and decide what is true and what isn't. In the world of the Bible, God decides what is true and has the final word on what "self-talk" we are supposed to allow in our minds each day. In the Bible, it is clear that Satan is "the father of lies," out to destroy you and me through those lies. He wants us to believe things that are not true because he knows lies cause psychological and spiritual misery. Satan will use anyone he can get his hands on to teach us lies, including parents, friends, teachers, politicians, and ministers. Try this on for size: Satan uses many pop psychology books to lead people away from the truth about who they really are and how to live life. That statement may sound paranoid or mean-spirited, but it is the truth.

In *The Lies We Believe,* I explore thirty different lies that destroy emotional and spiritual health—including "I must be perfect," "My worth is determined by my performance," and "God's love can be earned"—and then show how the truth in the Bible will defeat those lies. In *The Truths We Must Believe,* I examine twelve truths that I believe to be essential for emotional health, like "To err is human," "You reap what you sow," "Life is difficult," and "The virtue lies in the struggle, not the prize." Finally, *The Lies We Believe Workbook* is a twelve-week interactive program I designed to help people take specific steps to develop the mind of Christ. It combines material from both *The Lies We Believe* and *The Truths We Must Believe* with new material to enable the reader to experience truth at a deeper level in order to be set free from the bondage that lies create.

I mention these books not only to get you to buy them so I can be more famous (well, my wife and kids think I'm famous), get bigger royalty checks (maybe I'll get fifty dollars next time instead of the twenty-five I usually get), and live a more self-indulgent life (specifically, I would like to buy new floormats for my eight-year-old car), but to offer them as alternatives to the pop psychology books out there on "self-talk."

Earlier in this chapter, I gave you some examples of what Shad Helmstetter called negative and positive self-talk. Before I close this chapter, I would like to offer you some of my favorite "positive" and "negative" truths from the Bible. I do so, once again, to make the point that the issue isn't whether or not something is positive or negative but whether or not it is true. All of the biblical teachings listed below are important truths for emotional and spiritual health. While some self-talk authors would reject the first four truths because they are "negative," all of these truths need to become part of your mental "tape deck" so that you can become a mature person.

"The heart is deceitful above all things, and des-

perately wicked; who can know it?"[19] This is a critically important truth, one that seems lost on some
pop psychology authors. They tell us how wonderful
we are, yet the Bible tells us we have a huge problem
with deceiving ourselves and doing destructive things.
Most, if not all, of the self-affirmations that self-help
authors teach are examples not of what we need to
hear but of how self-deceived we are.

*"All have sinned and fall short of the glory of
God."*[20] This puts us in our proper place. Only God
is holy. We humans, although made in God's image,
fall *far* short of being like God in moral purity. This
truth is meant to keep us from becoming arrogant
about who we are and to create humility in us before
God.

*"Your adversary the devil walks about like a roar-
ing lion, seeking whom he may devour."*[21] You and I
have a real enemy in life named Satan, and he is on a
search-and-destroy mission the likes of which the
world has never seen. This isn't some biblical mumbo
jumbo, but a serious challenge to our foolish tendency
to think that we war only against things we can see
with our eyes or touch with our hands. Satan is alive
and well on planet earth, and he isn't taking any pris-
oners.

*"Come now, you rich, weep and howl for your
miseries that are coming upon you!"*[22] People who
worship wealth and use it to oppress others are in for
a rough comeuppance. Our country focuses so much

on the attainment of wealth, yet the Bible talks frequently about how enslaving wealth can be and how often it gets in the way of fully loving God.

"For God so loved the world that He gave His only begotten Son, that whoever believes in Him should not perish but have everlasting life."[23] Can you wrap your mind around the truth that God loves you to the point that He would give up His own Son on your behalf? It is an amazing love that would do that, isn't it? Also, isn't it radical to think about spending the rest of eternity with God? A perfect love and a perfect destiny. Two truths that transform the lives of those who believe them.

"And my God shall supply all your need according to His riches in glory by Christ Jesus."[24] We all have needs, and God is committed to meeting all of them. Some distort this into a "health-and-wealth" gospel, but what it really means is that God knows what you *truly* need and will not let you go without it. In troubled times like these, it's comforting to know that.

"There is therefore now no condemnation to those who are in Christ Jesus."[25] This truth ought to knock our socks off. We condemn ourselves, and others condemn us. Yet, in spite of all the wrongs we have done, God doesn't condemn us. Isn't it amazing that instead of the condemnation we deserve, God offers us His grace? What a liberating truth!

When the Bible says "As a man thinketh, so is he," it isn't teaching positive thinking, and it isn't suggesting you should always be happy. Developing the mind of Christ is a lifelong process of diligently working to replace the lies we believe with the truths we need to believe. It is a difficult task, one that will never be completely finished while we are still on earth.

May I encourage you to focus on developing the mind of Christ so that God can use the truth to set you free?

CHAPTER 7

Pop psychology myth #7:

STAYING "IN LOVE" IS THE KEY TO A GREAT RELATIONSHIP

Sometimes you need a scorecard to keep up with all the marital comings and goings of people in the movie industry. I was especially intrigued by the flap created a couple of years ago when actress Sharon Stone and producer Bill MacDonald fell in love during the filming of the movie, *Sliver.* All of this caused quite a sensation, partly because MacDonald had only been married for five months to his wife, Naomi, when he decided to leave her for Stone. Mrs. Mac-Donald, understandably distraught over all of this, had their marriage annulled and returned to her maiden name, Naomi Baka. Stone took tremendous heat in the popular press for helping to cause the breakup of MacDonald's marriage. Stone and Mac-Donald's affair didn't last, and they ended up parting ways.

The story doesn't end there, though. Enter Joe Eszterhas. Eszterhas is one of Hollywood's hottest screenwriters, getting as much as three million dollars a script. He has penned screenplays for *Basic Instinct* and *Sliver*, the kinds of movies that fit the term "no redeeming social value." It turns out that Eszterhas was a friend of both MacDonald and Baka when they were husband and wife and the affair with Stone took place. After MacDonald left Baka for Stone (which Eszterhas told him not to do) and the marriage had been annulled, Baka went along on a family vacation with Eszterhas, his wife of twenty-four years, Gerri, their children, and some friends to Hawaii.

Guess what happened next? You got it—Eszterhas and Baka fell in love during the vacation and he decided to leave his wife. Eszterhas himself probably couldn't have scripted this one any better! Baka, once an unfortunate victim, became a participant in helping to break up somebody else's marriage.

I read about all of this in the June 20, 1994, issue of *People*. What especially struck me about this whole situation was that "falling in love" was the primary basis for each person's actions. MacDonald and Stone fell in love with each other, and MacDonald suddenly left his wife of five months. Eszterhas and Baka fell in love with each other, and Eszterhas suddenly left his wife of twenty-four years. Falling in love is all some people seem to need to make a decision to spend the rest of their lives with another person, no matter who gets hurt in the process.

Yet, in spite of how much emotional pain has been caused by people "in love," one popular notion that is often trumpeted in pop psychology books is that staying "in love" is the key to a successful intimate relationship. Let's take a look at just one example.

Barbara DeAngelis is "one of America's foremost relationship experts." At least that is what her television infomercial tells us. She has written a number of books on the topic of intimate relationships, all best-sellers. DeAngelis, like so many of the people who write self-help books, appears to be deeply concerned about helping people make their lives better. She comes across as bright, articulate, funny, and warm; at least those were my impressions after reading her books and watching her award-winning infomercial.

One of Dr. DeAngelis's most popular books is entitled *How to Make Love All the Time*. First, let me say, the title alone wears me out. Okay, I know that she isn't talking about literally having sex all the time, at least I don't think she is (in her numerous references to "making love" in the book, she doesn't make it clear exactly what she is talking about). DeAngelis's title, I assume, refers to how to be involved in a relationship in which being in love is constant rather than infrequent or absent altogether.

In *How to Make Love All the Time,* DeAngelis states that "Life is about making love and about having lovemaking be spectacular, perfect, and unforgettable" and "Making love is probably the greatest high you can experience with another human being."[1] She contends that during lovemaking, "Suddenly the universe makes sense" and "suddenly you understand what you are doing here on this planet."[2] One of the sources she thanks for helping her see all this is the Maharishi Mahesh Yogi, who taught her that "the source of love and wisdom is inside me."

I think we have just entered the Twilight Zone and DeAngelis is playing Rod Serling! Sounds to me like she has an extremely romantic view of love and sees it as a highly emotional, druglike experience that has more to do with feelings than anything else. She even verifies this when she states in her book, "I was determined to discover the secrets of staying *in love*—to understand what created that *feeling* of being *'in love,'* and how to create that *feeling* everyday of my life."[3]

Please don't get me wrong on this. "Feeling in love" with somebody is a fantastic experience, but let me just as quickly say that it is also a shallow and unpredictable form of love, if it is love at all. We all know that "in love" feelings come and go and are often sexually motivated. If "in love" feelings were allowed to run the show in our intimate relationships, who of us would stay married for longer than a week?

DeAngelis goes on to make a number of points about how to "make love all the time" that I want to highlight. (Or should I say "lowlight"?)

"Passionate sex is a symptom of a passionate relationship."[4] It can be, but you can have "passionate sex" with someone with whom you have no real relationship. Ask someone who goes to prostitutes or who has had a one-night stand if it was passionate, and, if they are honest, many will tell you, "Yes." Sex can be passionate even in the absence of true intimacy.

I am not suggesting that passionate sex in the absence of an intimate relationship is good, because it isn't. I'm just saying that people sometimes fool themselves into thinking they have a good relationship just because the sex is "great." Passionate sex is greatest when it has true love as its foundation. If true love isn't underneath passionate sex, you are just using the person as an object for your own erotic pleasure. That's wrong, or at least it used to be back when the Bible was the authority on the matter.

"When you are loving, you feel alive, happy, and warm inside."[5] Yes, sometimes that is exactly how you feel. But I also feel "alive, happy, and warm" after I have had a great meal at my favorite restaurant. Real love had nothing to do with that.

The truth of the matter is that sometimes loving someone doesn't make you feel "happy and warm" inside. Ask Mother Teresa if her love for the people in Calcutta makes her feel happy and warm inside all the time. I doubt it. Most likely Mother Teresa feels alive each day (although I'm sure she also feels "dead" tired sometimes because of all the hard work she does), but her deep love for people who are in pain probably causes her as much sorrow and grief as it does happiness and warmth.

Sounds to me like DeAngelis is trying to sell people on being loving just for the positive payoffs that supposedly come. What about telling people that loving others will sometimes cost them dearly? "Be loving, and sometimes you will feel tremendous pain!" Do you think very many people want to hear that? Probably not. Yet, the deepest kind of love is that which enables a person to be willing to hurt, even die, for the benefit of another.

"If you can't get your needs met from one source, you are responsible for locating another. In this way, you are always self-sufficient and self-reliant."[6] With this attitude, you see people as a "source" (object) that you go to to get your needs met rather than as human beings who also have needs. It turns people into gas pumps: if the gas pump you are at is dry or doesn't have enough to fill your tank, move on to the next one to see if it has enough to give you. What about focusing just as much on what you can do to help put gas in the tank of that person who is dry or low on fuel?

Also, how in the world can people be "self-sufficient and self-reliant" if they look to others as the source of getting their needs met? Going from one person to another to get your needs met doesn't make you *self*-sufficient. In fact, self-sufficiency is a completely bogus notion. None of us is self-sufficient because none of us is capable of meeting all of our own needs. What we are supposed to be is appropriately interdependent, looking to God and each other for help to meet needs we can't meet on our own.

"A relationship between two people is an interplay of three energy fields: the mental, emotional, and physical energies of one person interact with those same energies of the partner."[7] Energy fields? Sounds like we are headed back into the "you can even see a glow around me" nonsense. More important, notice what DeAngelis leaves out of the types of "energy fields" around which people interact: the spiritual. I will suggest later in this chapter that it is the most important aspect of intimacy.

Before I focus on the biblical view of intimacy in relationships, I want to mention one other aspect of what DeAngelis teaches her readers in *How to Make Love All the Time*. She believes that there are three criteria for a successful relationship: 1) You give each other the love you both need; 2) You are compatible; and 3) You are willing to grow together in the same direction at the same speed.[8] If these criteria are not met, she encourages readers to realize that it is time to move on and get a new partner. DeAngelis practices what she preaches, ending one of her five marriages because she changed and needed someone who would be "compatible with the 'new' me."[9]

Let me suggest that a relationship can still be quite successful and not meet these three criteria. First, I certainly agree that meeting each other's needs is critically important in building an intimate relationship. But many of us enter marriage quite deficient in meeting another person's needs. There has to be a lot of slack in a relationship at first, since most of us have to learn how to love another person and lose the "give me the love I need right now or I'm out of here" attitude.

Second, I agree that being compatible is important in a relationship. When you are looking for a mate, you want to try and find one with whom you are reasonably compatible in terms of values, beliefs, goals, and so on. But no two people are completely compatible. In fact, some of the best marriages around involve people who are quite different from each other. The key issue here is learning to handle the differences well. "Different" doesn't mean "bad," and mature couples who are very different from each other see their differences as a plus. These couples actually complement each other.

Finally, growing together in the same direction and at the same speed is a delusion. Couples just don't grow like that. Successful relationships are those that learn how to handle the ebb and flow of each person growing (and regressing) at different rates over time. Sure, ideally, you want to be "on the same page" with your partner as much as possible, but getting out of a marriage because your partner isn't "compatible with the 'new' me" is a sure prescription for having more marital partners than Elizabeth Taylor.

Let's turn now to what the Bible has to say about marriage and intimate relationships.

. . . .

The Bible, Marriage, and Intimate Relationships

What is the first example of God being "negative" in the Bible?

Let me give you a hint: It occurs in the book of Genesis. Need another hint? Okay. It concerned the first person He created, a man named Adam. Still don't know? Well, let me set the stage for you.

In the first chapter of Genesis, God initiates the greatest construction project ever, something that would make building the Taj Mahal look like child's play. He creates the earth and water and says, "It is good." God creates the grass and trees and says, "It is good." God creates the heavens and says, "It is good." God creates all the living creatures and says, "It is good." God makes the first man, Adam, and says, "It is good." So far, so good.

Then, God looks at Adam, sees that he is alone, and says for the very first time in recorded history, "It is not good." Isn't it interesting that the first time God sees something that isn't to His liking it has to do with a human being lacking intimacy with another human being?

On the surface, Adam appeared to have everything he needed for an "exceptional and worthwhile" life. He walked intimately with the God of the universe every day. Everything on earth was his to have dominion over. The world he lived in was crime-free, pollution-free, and hassle-free. And yet, one thing was horribly wrong with Adam's situation. God saw what it was, was greatly bothered by it, and boldly acted to remedy it. He created a helpmate for Adam and started the institution of marriage, and things have never been the same since.

What concerned God about Adam's situation is the same thing He is concerned about with you and me each day—our intimate relationships. First and foremost, God wants us to have an intimate relationship with Him. That "vertical" relationship is the most important one of all. If it isn't in good shape, everything else is in trouble, no matter how good things may appear to be. Yet, it is clear from the Genesis account that even if we have a close, intimate relationship with the Creator, which Adam did, we still need to be intimate with other people in order for things to be truly "good."

DeAngelis and other relationship "experts" talk about relationship intimacy as being anchored in meeting each other's mental, emotional, and physical needs. Yet, how can anyone talk about "making love work" in an intimate relationship if they divorce the discussion from God, who created relationships?

Yes, I know I'm being rigid here, but the fact of the matter is that God masterminded marriage. He came up with the idea. Wouldn't you think that the God who made people and who created marriage would know more about both than anyone else? How any of us could hope to figure out marriage and other intimate human relationships apart from God is a mystery to me.

Let's examine some of what the Bible says about intimate relationships and how its advice differs from some of the input that DeAngelis offered in *How to Make Love All the Time*.

The Bible says, "Therefore a man shall leave his father and mother and be joined to his wife, and they shall become one flesh."[10] "One flesh"—what a powerful image for the inseparable union that a man and a woman are supposed to have with each other in marriage! Put the idea of "one flesh" together with the following passage where Christ, talking about marriage, said: "So then, they are no longer two but one flesh. Therefore what God has joined together, let not man separate."[11] You can see from these two statements that God is pretty serious about marriage, that He sees it as a deeply intimate, lifelong, monogamous commitment.

Contrast that biblical teaching with DeAngelis's decision to end one of her five marriages because her husband was no longer "compatible with the 'new' me." Wouldn't it be interesting if instead of getting advice from the Maharishi Mahesh Yogi she came face to face with Christ for guidance on her marriage? I believe Christ would have told her to stay in the marriage and work on becoming a more deeply loving person.

Okay, so the Bible teaches that marriage is a once-and-forever relationship. What does the Bible teach about how marriage is supposed to work? First, the Bible teaches that husbands are supposed to love their wives "just as Christ loved the church."[12] Think about that for a minute. Christ loved the church so much that He died for its well-being. There is no greater sacrifice than that. Christ gave His all for the church, and, likewise, husbands are to give their all for their wives.

Another biblical teaching that has tremendous implications for marital intimacy says, "Husbands, likewise, dwell with them with understanding, giving honor to the wife, as to the weaker vessel, and as being heirs together of the grace of life, that your prayers may not be hindered."[15] How many marriage counselors have heard one or both partners say, "He/she is so inconsiderate and shows me no respect!"

and "He/she doesn't really understand who I am!"? A tremendous amount of marital pain comes from a lack of consideration, respect, and understanding shown by one or both partners to the other. Good marriage counseling works diligently to help couples become more considerate, respectful, and understanding toward each other.

Before I go on, let me address the issue of wives being referred to as the "weaker" partner. I personally believe that this is simply a reference to sheer physical strength, not character, moral fortitude, or intelligence. Men, in general, are physically stronger than women. Far too many husbands have used both the "wives submit" and "weaker vessel" statements in the Bible to justify treating their wives badly. That is horribly wrong.

Let's take the biblical notion "be considerate" a little further. In marriage (and other intimate relationships) we are to understand our spouses as deeply as possible, being sensitive to who they are and how they are "wired." We are to know what their physical, emotional, and spiritual needs are, and, with God's help, meet those needs as best we can. We are to see our partners as God's creation, treating them with the respect and dignity that go along with that status.

Hey, what about all this "needs" stuff? Isn't it selfish to focus on our needs? Shouldn't we ignore our own needs and focus only on our partner's needs?

Those are good questions, and they deserve good answers.

First, the Bible does in fact teach that people have needs. Christ said, "And when you pray, do not use vain repetitions as the heathen do. For they think that they will be heard for their many words. Therefore do not be like them. For your Father knows the things you have need of before you ask Him."[16] God not only knows what you need, He promises to meet your needs. "And my God shall supply all your need according to His riches in glory by Christ Jesus."[17] From these two passages alone, I think it is safe to conclude that it is okay to have needs and that God has promised to meet those needs.

What does all this have to do with intimate relationships? Well, one of the primary ways God meets our needs is through our spouse. When two people marry and become "one flesh," God desires to use that relationship to meet many of the physical, mental, emotional, and spiritual needs of each person. One challenge all of us face as marriage partners is to know what those various needs are and to make ourselves available to God to be used by Him to meet those needs in each other. I am not suggesting that meeting each other's needs should become our central focus in life, but it is clear in the Bible that marital oneness is fundamentally tied to being just as concerned about meeting your partner's needs as you are with having your own needs met.

What are some of the needs referred to here? In the physical arena, they range from nonsexual touching and holding to sexual intercourse. In the mental arena, we have needs for knowledge, insight, and understanding. In the emotional arena, our needs include everything from appreciation to comfort to respect. In the spiritual arena, our needs include God's love, discipline, grace, and forgiveness.

Now, you might be thinking, "All this is nice and good, but my marriage is a mess and I want out!" You're right, all the things I have mentioned are "nice and good" and represent how God wants things to be in marriage. But our marriages are often a whole different story. Instead of living in a respectful and understanding manner with each other, we often show little regard for the other person. Instead of caring as much about the other person's needs as we do our own, we often selfishly demand that our needs get met first before we reciprocate. Instead of seeing marriage as a lifelong, monogamous, "for better or for worse" commitment, we replace partners like we replace burned-out lightbulbs.

Yes, there is a "nice and good" way that marriage is supposed to be, but so few of us actually do it that way. Like the apostle Paul, we often find ourselves "not doing what we should, and doing what we shouldn't" in life, and this problem is especially true in marriage. Instead of following God's route through marriage, we go our own route, based on what we feel will reduce our pain in the quickest and easiest way. Yet, is going out and finding a new partner the solution to our marital problems? Does that truly solve anything? Sure, we might feel happier, but do we mature into more loving people? In most cases, the truth of the matter is that we remain the same immature, unloving people we were in the previous relationships.

It is truly an act of courage when couples honestly face why they aren't getting along and start to deal with the real issues that are causing their problems. Think about how much a husband and wife would actually grow if they tried to do this rather than jettison each other when they no longer feel "in love." Please don't hear me saying that a person should tolerate physical, emotional, or spiritual abuse in marriage. That is never right or helpful. I'm just saying that we often seek quick fixes for marital pain that usually don't work rather than seek solutions that may take longer and be more painful but that really last.

In its deepest form, "Love suffers long and is kind; love does not envy; love does not parade itself, is not puffed up; does not behave rudely, does not seek its own, is not provoked, thinks no evil; does not rejoice in iniquity, but rejoices in the truth; bears all things, believes all things, hopes all things, endures all things. Love never fails."[18] Marriage tests all that.

There is a very old joke that says there are three rings in marriage: the engagement ring, the wedding ring, and suffering. There is an element of truth to that statement. Marriage is going to involve suffering because, like a strenuous workout at the gym, it pushes you to become better (more mature and loving) than you are. Specifically, marriage involves learning to lay down your life for the well-being of another person, just as Christ did for us. This doesn't mean being a victim. It does mean learning to love even when it hurts to do so.

For a more in-depth look at marital intimacy from a biblical perspective, may I recommend that you read Larry Crabb's *The Marriage Builder,* Ed Wheat's *Love Life for Every Married Couple,* R. C. Sproul's *The Intimate Marriage,* and *The Pursuit of Intimacy* by David and Teresa Ferguson and Chris and Holly Thurman.

God created marriage, has a plan for how marriage is supposed to work, and deeply desires to be actively involved in our marriages so that they can be truly intimate places.

When God created marriage, He did so out of a desire for us to have the best lives possible. Before Adam and Eve sinned, they enjoyed a relationship of perfect harmony, one that was free from shame, free from anger, free from hurt, and free from destructive games. They were "one" across all dimensions of life: physical, mental, emotional, and spiritual. After they sinned, sadly, all this changed for the worse.

Since the time of Adam and Eve, all couples have

struggled to reenter the Garden of Eden and to find the "oneness" they were meant to have. None of us will ever have what Adam and Eve experienced before they sinned, but with God's help we can have a rich taste of what it was like.

God, as the source of love (contrary to DeAngelis's assertion that the source of love is inside each of us), wants very badly to be allowed back into our marriages so He can show us how to make them work. We can resist His help, or yield to it.

Want to "make love all the time"? Turn to God—who is love—for help, and you have a legitimate shot at having a truly loving, intimate relationship. Leave God out, and what you are likely to make all the time is war, not love.

CHAPTER 8

Pop psychology myth #8:

YOU HAVE
UNLIMITED
POWER AND
POTENTIAL

Howard Hughes was an amazing man by human standards. He broke airplane speed records, designed and built his own planes, made motion pictures, created one of the world's most successful companies, made millions, and dated and married several beautiful women. It seemed he could do anything he set his mind to. Yet, while Howard Hughes was once one of the richest, most successful men in the world, he also seemed to be one of the most miserable. Alan McGinnis, in his book, *The Friendship Factor,* describes the sad plight of Howard Hughes this way:

> Howard Hughes was the world's ultimate mystery—
> so secretive, so reclusive, so enigmatic, that for more

than fifteen years no one could say for certain that he was alive, much less how he looked or behaved. . . . He lived a sunless, joyless, half-lunatic life. In his later years he fled from one resort hotel to another— Las Vegas, Nicaragua, Acapulco—and his physical appearance became odder and odder. His straggly beard hung down to his waist and his hair reached to the middle of his back. His fingernails were two inches long, and his toenails hadn't been trimmed for so long they resembled corkscrews . . .

Hughes often said, "Every man has his price or a guy like me couldn't exist," yet no amount of money bought the affection of his associates. Most of his employees who have broken their silence report their disgust for him.[1]

For Howard Hughes as a young, energetic man, the sky seemed to be the limit, and many self-help books teach that it is. Frequently passed along as truth in many self-help books is the notion that human beings have unlimited power and potential to do or be anything they want in life. In our day and age, we admire men and women like Howard Hughes, at least until their lives start to self-destruct because they have been so consumed with themselves and their power.

Perhaps the most popular spokesperson for the "power and potential" movement in America today is Anthony Robbins. If you watch television, I am sure you have seen his infomercials. They are slickly produced and offer numerous testimonials from a variety of "common" people, as well as famous celebrities, concerning how Robbins and his teachings have dramatically changed their lives for the better.

In the infomercials, it is hard not to like Robbins. He is bright, articulate, handsome, and caring, and he appears to dedicate 110 percent of himself to helping people utilize their talents and abilities. Robbins speaks with great conviction about unlocking one's potential and creating a more fulfilling life, and he seems to practice what he preaches. On top of all that, Robbins spends his own time and money in numerous charitable endeavors. So, what's there not to like?

The problem is that in his desire to help people live more meaningful and more enjoyable lives, Robbins turns them into all-powerful gods. The back of his best-selling book, *Unlimited Power,* reads: "Yes, you can do, have, achieve, and create anything you want out of life. Anthony Robbins has proved it." We don't actually find out *how* Robbins has "proved" this. I guess we are supposed to take his word for it. In another of his best-sellers, *Awaken the Giant Within,* Robbins states that his life's quest has been to "get each of us to remember and use the unlimited power that lies sleeping within us all." He goes on to suggest that "the resources we need to turn our dreams into reality are within us, merely waiting for the day when we decide to wake up and claim our birthright."[2]

Robbins wants us to believe that we can "do, have,

achieve, and create anything" in life. Is that true? Can you, I, or anyone else on the planet actually accomplish anything we want to? Anything? If I completely dedicate myself to the task of running a mile in world-record time, could I do it? If I completely dedicate myself to painting a masterpiece, could I do it? If I completely dedicate myself to being loved by everyone, could I do it? If I completely dedicate myself to being the best psychologist in the world, could I do it? According to Robbins, the answer is one big "Yes!"

At the risk of sounding negative and self-deprecating, the answer to each of those questions in my life has been, is, and always will be one big "No!" No matter how completely I dedicate myself, I will *never* break the world record in the mile, *never* paint a masterpiece, *never* be loved by everyone, and *never* be the world's greatest psychologist. These things are out of my reach for one simple reason—I am not equipped with the talents, abilities, and skills that would allow me to achieve them. That isn't being negative or self-defeating; it's being realistic.

On the other hand, it would be defeatist and unnecessarily self-limiting to think that I could never run a mile in under six minutes, never paint something my youngest daughter, Kelly, would like, never be loved by certain people, or never be a better psychologist. Those things are within the reach of my abilities and help motivate me to keep striving to improve. However, the idea that you or I can do *anything* we want is complete, absolute nonsense. It raises the standard for individual performance so high that frustration, disappointment, and hopelessness are the inevitable results.

According to Robbins, not only is your potential limitless, but also you have "unlimited power" residing inside you to enable you to achieve your potential. You are powerful enough in and of yourself to do whatever you think you can do. Is that really true? Do you know anyone who has unlimited power? Most of the people I know can barely program their VCR or keep their checkbooks balanced! Whatever power we personally possess is finite, not infinite. Yes, I know people who are powerful by human standards, but their power is still quite limited and can be taken away from them in the blink of an eye. Teaching people that they have unlimited power and potential turns them into self-contained deities. It is one of the scariest and deadliest of all the teachings in self-help books.

Anthony Robbins isn't alone in his belief that we are sleeping giants who can achieve anything we choose to. Wayne Dyer believes it as well. One of Dyer's biggest best-sellers is entitled *The Sky's the Limit.* Dyer believes that the term, "the sky's the limit," is "most true when applied to the potentials of human beings" and that the world is in the mess that it is because "individuals have been blind to the limitlessness of their own potentials."[3] He seems to believe that nothing less than the future of humankind depends on whether or not we tap into our unlimited human potential: "Nothing can be more important to me or to us than the legacy of mental health and the belief in the limitless potential of human beings which we bequeath to the next and all future generations."[4]

What is required for you to tap into your full potential? Dyer says that "you must allow yourself to think of yourself as perfect if you are ever to reach your full potential as a human being."[5] He goes on to suggest that "the essence of your perfection is in your own ability to look at yourself, accept what you see as perfect in the present moment, and then be able to grow into something quite different, *but still perfect*" (his emphasis).[6]

While appearing on a national television show, Dyer describes an encounter he had with a woman. Apparently, Dyer said something about how important it is to see yourself as perfect, and the woman had the nerve to ask him how it felt to be perfect. Dyer takes the woman to task for believing "that it is some kind of sin to think of yourself as perfect" or "that you should be dissatisfied with yourself and always striving to try to fulfill someone else's idea of what it is to be perfect." He suggests that "she probably thinks only God is perfect."[7]

It is a delusion for Dyer to think that he is perfect as he is because the simple truth of the matter is that he is not. And he never will be perfect. That is why it is appropriate to be "dissatisfied with yourself" to a certain degree. That doesn't mean hating yourself or beating yourself up for your deficiencies. It does mean that we admit that imperfections exist (actually, abound) in each of us and that we work on improving them. As far as "always striving to fulfill someone else's idea of what it means to be perfect," there *is* someone whose idea of perfection needs to be what all of us are striving for (more on that "someone" and His ideas about pursuing perfection later). Finally, if that woman thinks only God is perfect, I think she's pretty smart.

"Self-talk" expert, Shad Helmstetter, agrees with Anthony Robbins and Wayne Dyer. He is on the bandwagon when it comes to the idea that we humans can pull off anything we want to. In *What to Say When You Talk to Your Self,* Dr. Helmstetter says we need to tell ourselves these nuggets of "truth" each day:

- "I can do anything I believe I can do."
- "I know that I can accomplish anything I choose."
- "There is no challenge I can't conquer."
- "I am an exceptional human being. My goals and my incredible belief in myself turn my goals into reality."

Helmstetter suggests that you try reading these statements "to yourself in front of a mirror each morning for the next few days!"[8] What kind of people would we be if we stood in front of a mirror everyday and told ourselves nonsense like this? We would all suffer from delusions of grandeur that would make our lives absolutely miserable! Can you imagine a world full of people like that?

Well, enough of what pop psychology has to say on human potential and personal power. Let's see what the Bible has to say about both.

· · · · · · · · · · · ·

The Bible, Human Potential, and Personal Power

There is *nothing* in the Bible to suggest that we humans have *unlimited* power and potential to achieve anything we choose. *Nothing.* Even though we are made in the image of God[9] and created a little bit lower than the angels,[10] we are not infinite and limitless in our capabilities. There is only one person who has unlimited power, and it isn't you or me.

The issue in the Bible isn't "Do people have unlimited power and potential?," but "How will people use the finite power and potential they have?" Unfortunately, our "bent" toward sin means that we are much more likely to use our power and potential in selfish, self-destructive ways rather than in selfless, constructive ways. This is why the Bible raises perhaps the single most important question any of us will ever be asked: Are we going to choose God's way or our own?

"I call heaven and earth as witnesses today against you, that I have set before you life and death, blessing and cursing; therefore choose life, that both you and your descendants may live; that you may love the Lord your God, that you may obey His voice, and that you may cling to Him."[11]

Are we going to turn our lives over to God and let Him mold us into mature people who are powerful on His behalf, or are we going to keep running our lives on our own power and harden into immature people who misuse the power we have? God has laid those two options before each of us. There is no third option. You are either on God's path or your own. Your potential is either being used for good or for evil. You are either being powerful for God or powerful for yourself.

This is why I have such a hard time with human-potential gurus who leave God completely out of the picture. How can you tap into your true potential or be powerful in the right ways if you leave the true source of your potential and power out of the picture? God made you with potential and has the power to help you use it properly. Apart from Him any effort to reach your full potential and be powerful in life is ultimately meaningless. As the psalmist put it, "Unless the Lord builds the house, They labor in vain who build it."[12]

The Bible talks a great deal about God's awesome power, whereas most self-help books focus almost exclusively on the awesomeness of human power. Read these statements about God's power and see how they compare to the power we humans have:

- "Great is our Lord, and mighty in power; / His understanding is infinite."[13]
- "He has made the earth by His power, / He has established the world by His wisdom, / And has stretched out the heavens at His discretion."[14]
- "O LORD God of our fathers, are You not God in heaven, and do You not rule over all the kingdoms of the nations, and in Your hand is there not power and might, so that no one is able to withstand You?"[15]

Whatever talents and abilities we *do* have are from God. That is why the Bible says, "He who glories, let him glory in the LORD"[16] and "In God we boast all day long."[17] Whatever potential you have and power you posses, it isn't yours. You may take credit for what your hands have accomplished, but you are deluding yourself if you think the power and potential came from you.

Let me tell you a story to make the point. King Nebuchadnezzar once ruled over the greatest kingdom of his day, Babylon. He was the king who became angry with Shadrach, Meshach, and Abednego because they wouldn't worship a golden image and he had them thrown into a fiery furnace. They came out of the furnace in great shape (because of divine intervention), and Nebuchadnezzar ended up singing the praises of the God who delivered them from a horrible death.

However, King Nebuchadnezzar's appreciation for the God of Shadrach, Meshach, and Abednego didn't last very long. He believed his own power was responsible for the greatness of the kingdom of Babylon. Nebuchadnezzar, in other words, was full of himself. He was, in his own mind, God's equal if not superior.

In the midst of all this, Nebuchadnezzar had a dream that terrified him. Initially he couldn't find anyone who was able to interpret the dream. Then he turned to Daniel (the lions' den hero), who told him some pretty bad news. The dream was a message from God: Unless Nebuchadnezzar repented of his pride and acknowledged that it is God who is sovereign over the kingdoms of the world and who gives them to whom He wants, Nebuchadnezzar would lose his kingdom and be reduced to an insane, grass-eating beast.

Twelve months went by (God is very patient), and Nebuchadnezzar hadn't repented of his pride. One day, while walking on the roof of the royal palace, Nebuchadnezzar said to himself, "Is not this the great Babylon I have built as the royal residence, by my mighty power and for the glory of my majesty?" (Robbins, Dyer, and Helmstetter would be so proud!)

God wasn't proud, though. God immediately put

the pedal to the medal and drove Nebuchadnezzar from his kingdom and out into the fields to eat grass like a wild animal. Nebuchadnezzar's body was "drenched with dew," his hair grew long "like the feathers of an eagle," and his fingernails grew "like the claws of a bird." Nebuchadnezzar's sanity was taken from him and he spent the next *seven years* of his life this way. Sounds like Howard Hughes, doesn't it?

At the end of the seven years, Nebuchadnezzar's sanity was restored and he praised the very God that he had earlier prided as his equal. Listen to Nebuchadnezzar's words from Daniel 4:34–35; they should certainly be our own each day:

> For his dominion is an everlasting
> dominion,
> And His kingdom is from generation to
> generation.
> All the inhabitants of the earth are
> reputed as nothing;
> He does according to His will in the
> army of heaven
> And among the inhabitants of the earth.
> No one can restrain His hand
> Or say to Him, "What have You done?"

Amazing transformation, wasn't it? From an arrogant king to a humble man praising the King of Kings for allowing him to rule over Babylon.

Helmstetter advised us to stand in front of a mirror everyday and repeat things like "I can do anything I believe I can do . . . ", "I know that I can accomplish anything I choose . . . ", and "There is no challenge I can't conquer . . ." These are the kinds of statements that were going through Nebuchadnezzar's mind prior to becoming a grass-eating maniac.

I'd like to challenge Helmstetter, Robbins, and Dyer—and anyone else who believes that human beings have unlimited potential and power. If you can do anything you believe you can do, then try keeping the Ten Commandments perfectly. If you can accomplish anything you choose to, try walking on water or calming a stormy sea. If there is no challenge you can't overcome, bring someone back from the dead. If you can turn all of your goals into reality, turn water into wine.

One final challenge for anyone who believes in unlimited human power and potential. Try to get into heaven on your own merits. Try to live such a perfect life that a perfectly holy God would be satisfied and would allow you into His heavenly home to have eternal fellowship with Him. Remember, you are going to have to be *completely* free from *any* moral stain your whole life to get into heaven on your own merits. You will have to live life just like Jesus Christ lived it—from birth to grave.

If Helmstetter, Robbins, Dyer, or anyone else were to respond to my challenges, they would have only one of two choices. They could take the route of saying that those things I have challenged them to do are not things they want to do. They don't want to obey the Ten Commandments, raise the dead, or turn water into wine. That would be the easy way out, though, wouldn't it? I would then want to ask them, "Why? Why don't you want to do these things? They are, after all, wonderful, inspiring, worthwhile things to do."

The other option, the one that would require a great deal of honesty, would be for them to admit that they can't do these things because they don't have the power or potential to do them in their own strength. These are things that show us—prove to us—we don't have unlimited power or potential. Christ did them because He was God-man. Human beings can't pull them off through their own power. We can only do them if God does them through us using His power.

While all of the human potential and personal power prophets of today tell us how powerful we are and that "the sky's the limit" in terms of what we can achieve in life, there is only one person in the universe with unlimited power and potential: God. Whatever power and potential we have come from Him. Instead of standing on our own personal palace roofs and pounding our chests with pride over how many wonderful things we have done, we all need to get on our knees and thank God for doing good through us and in spite of who we are.

CHAPTER 9

Pop psychology myth #9:

YOUR HAPPINESS IS THE MOST IMPORTANT THING IN LIFE

W hat do you really want out of life?

Very few questions are more important for us to answer during our time on this earth. Yet, pose this question to ten different people and you are likely to get a pretty broad range of answers.

- "I just want to be married and have a family."
- "I want to be financially secure."
- "I want to make the world a better place."

Perhaps one of the most frequent answers to this question is "I just want to be happy." French philosopher Blaise Pascal wrote:

> All men seek happiness. This is without exception.
> Whatever different means they employ, they all tend
> to this end. The cause of some going to war, and
> others avoiding it, is the same desire in both,
> attending with different views. The will never takes
> the least step but to this objective. This is the motive
> of every man, even of those who hang themselves.[1]

Being happy is emphasized in many self-help books. In fact, some of these books go so far as to suggest that being happy is the single most important thing in life, something we should strive for whatever the cost may be. "If something is making you unhappy, stop doing it; and if something makes you happy, go for it" seems to be the central theme of more than a few personal-growth books.

Robert Ringer wrote a book in 1977 entitled *Looking Out for Number One,* which spent more than a year on the *New York Times* best-seller list. It is still in your local bookstore today. In the book's introduction, Ringer tells us that "my sole reason for writing this book was to make as much money as possible."[2] Well, at least he's honest!

In *Looking Out for Number One,* Ringer shares his view that "looking out for Number One is the conscious, rational effort to spend as much time doing those things which bring you the greatest amount of pleasure and less time on those which cause pain."[3] He also states that "looking out for Number One is important because it leads to a simple, uncomplicated life in which you spend more time doing those things which give you the greatest amount of pleasure."[4] Pleasure, pleasure, pleasure. "When you boil it all down," says Ringer, "I think that's what everyone's main objective in life really is—to feel good."[5] He also notes that "we sometimes lose sight of the fact that our primary objective is really to be as happy as possible and that all our other objectives, great and small, are only a means to that end."[6]

Ringer goes on to let us know that happiness can and will take different forms for different people. "Even if everyone exercised good reason before acting, each of us would seek his happiness in a different way."[7] Some people, he suggests, might seek happiness through being knowledgeable, others by accumulating great wealth. How can you tell if you are doing well in your effort to be happy? "If you're feelin' good, don't ask questions," Ringer answers.[8]

The big enemy of happiness, according to Ringer, is the "absolute moralist." The absolute moralist is any human being who tells you what is right for you. Morality is "a very personal and private matter," according to Ringer.[9] You should avoid in your life any person who acts as though he or she knows what is right for you. "You should concern yourself only with whether looking out for Number One is moral from your own rational, aware viewpoint."[10] I wonder if Ringer understands that this mindset—that morality is "a very personal and private matter"—is what leads to the existence of the Adolf Hitlers of the world?

After telling us that no one has the right to tell us what is right for us, Ringer goes on *to tell us what is right for us:* "Man's primary moral duty lies in the pursuit of pleasure so long as he does not forcibly interfere with the rights of others."[11] Forcible interference isn't acceptable because "it's simply not in your best interest."[12]

Ringer is not alone in his focus on happiness. Wayne Dyer, in *Your Erroneous Zones,* enlightens us that "Happiness is the natural condition of being a person";[13] his book, he says, is a "pleasant approach to achieving happiness."[14] He tells us that in order to understand how to live effectively you just have to be "committed to your own happiness."[15] Dyer stresses the "ability to choose happiness or at least not to choose unhappiness at any given moment of your life" as the key issue in life.[16] Apparently Dyer would never think that choosing to be unhappy might be the most sane, rational, constructive thing to do given certain circumstances.

Peter McWilliams, in his book *Life 101,* has a simple (or should I say "simplistic"?) approach to being happy. According to McWilliams, "Our lives are full of happy things we can think happy thoughts about. If we run out of those, there are books, music, and movies full of happy thoughts. All we have to do is focus on the happy things to think happy thoughts, which will make us happy. That's all."[17] (I would love to see him sell this line of thinking in poverty-stricken or war-torn countries where people's lives are in danger everyday.)

Is wanting to be happy inherently wrong or selfish? Personally, I don't think so. I agree with John Piper, in *Desiring God,* when he says "The longing to be happy is a universal human experience, and it is good, not sinful"[18] and "We should never try to deny or resist our longing to be happy, as though it were a bad impulse. Instead we should seek to intensify this longing and nourish it with whatever will provide the deepest and most enduring satisfaction."[19]

So what's the problem? The problem in certain self-help books is twofold: 1) the authors approach happiness as if it is the most important thing in life, and 2) they suggest we can find true happiness only in pleasurable things. Let me explain.

First, whenever we make our happiness the most important thing, we become even more selfish and self-absorbed. We see people only in terms of how we can use them to make us happy, and we move away from focusing on how to serve others.

Second, when we attach our happiness to pleasurable things, we set ourselves up to be unhappy. When you ask people what it would take to make them happy, they will usually respond by saying that something external will do the trick—getting a new house, earning a college degree, getting a promotion, paying off a debt, taking a trip. Not only do a lot of us buy into the idea that pleasurable things can truly make us happy, but we also believe that *more* of them will make us even *happier*. Yet, when our happiness is solely tied to externals, we are doomed. Pleasurable externals go up and down, and we will go up and down with them.

George Will once said, "To visit a bookstore is to feel misgivings about universal literacy, which has produced a mass market for hundreds of profoundly sad books on achieving happiness."[20] I couldn't agree with him more. It is sad that we are so obsessed with happiness, and it is even sadder that we buy so many misguided books on how to achieve it. Is there something more important than our happiness that we need to be seeking? Let me allow the Bible speak to those questions.

· · · · · · · · · · · ·

The Bible and Happiness

In the Bible happiness and unhappiness are usually mentioned in the context of some external circumstance. In Matthew, a man who owns a hundred sheep was happy because he found the one that was lost.[21] In Esther, the Jews experienced a "time of happiness" related to an edict issued by King Xerxes that protected them from the evil that Haman wanted to do to them.[22] Job said that "my eyes will never see happiness again" after God allowed Satan to take his family, property, and health from him.[23] Solomon wrote, "In the day of prosperity be joyful,"[24] and encouraged, "Rejoice, O young man, in your youth."[25] Jonah was "very happy" about a vine that God provided for him as shade but became so unhappy when it withered, he wanted to die.[26] Happiness, at least as far as the Bible is concerned, is tied to happenstance. Because it is, happiness is not something we are supposed to feel all the time.

The Bible even describes one of the best case examples of a person who purposely went out to find pleasure and happiness. If Robert Ringer is correct when he suggests that we should do everything we can to maximize our pleasure and minimize our pain, this guy would have made him very proud, at least up to a certain point. That man's name was Solomon. He was the epitome of a "Looking Out for Number One" kind of guy. In fact, no one prior to Solomon, and probably no one since, had pulled off the combination of knowledge, wealth, power, and pleasure he did. Let's let Solomon describe it:

> I made my works great, I built myself houses, and planted myself vineyards. I made myself gardens and orchards, and I planted all kinds of fruit trees in them. I made myself water pools from which to water the growing trees of the grove. I acquired male and female servants, and had servants born in my house. Yes, I had greater possessions of herds and flocks than all

who were in Jerusalem before me. I also gathered for myself silver and gold and the special treasures of kings and of the provinces. I acquired male and female singers, the delights of the sons of men, and musical instruments of all kinds. So I became great and excelled more than all who were before me in Jerusalem. Also my wisdom remained with me. Whatever my eyes desired I did not keep from them. I did not withhold my heart from any pleasure.[27]

Solomon not only looked out for Number One, he was Number One. Now, you would think that Solomon would be the happiest guy around, right? Not so. Solomon, it would appear, was one of the unhappiest people ever to set foot on the earth. Listen to him tell it in his own words:

> "Vanity of vanities," says the Preacher;
> "Vanity of vanities, all is vanity." . . .
> All things are full of labor;
> Man cannot express it.
> The eye is not satisfied with seeing,
> Nor the ear filled with hearing. . . .
> I have seen all the works that are done under the sun; and indeed, all is vanity and grasping for the wind. . . .
> I said in my heart, "Come now, I will test you with mirth; therefore enjoy pleasure"; but surely this also was vanity. I said of laughter—"Madness!"; and of mirth, "What does it accomplish?" . . .

Then I looked on all the works that my
    hands had done
And on the labor in which I had toiled;
And indeed all was vanity and grasping
    for the wind.
There was no profit under the sun. . . .

Therefore I hated life because the work that was
done under the sun was distressing to me, for all is
vanity and grasping for the wind. Then I hated all
my labor in which I had toiled under the sun, because
I must leave it to the man who will come after me.
And who knows whether he will be wise or a fool?
Yet he will rule over all my labor in which I toiled and
in which I have shown myself wise under the sun. . . .

For what has man for all his labor, and for the
striving of his heart with which he has toiled under
the sun? For all his days are sorrowful, and his work
burdensome; even in the night his heart takes no rest.
This also is vanity. . . .

He who loves silver will not be satisfied
    with silver;
Nor he who loves abundance, with increase.
This also is vanity.
When goods increase,
They increase who eat them;
So what profit have the owners
Except to see them with their eyes?[28]

If all of these statements were coming from a
"loser," someone who finished last in the race to be

Number One, we might call it sour grapes. Instead, the "king of the hill" peered down from the top of the heap and proclaimed it a meaningless chasing after the wind. Maybe the things that bring us the greatest amount of pleasure in the moment aren't the best things for us in the long run. Maybe happiness shouldn't be the main goal of life. Could be that making happiness our main goal is the surest way to be miserably unhappy.

Solomon certainly would agree. After all that he achieved, after all the wisdom he gained, after all the power he wielded, Solomon said that life really comes down to one thing: "Let us hear the conclusion of the whole matter: Fear God and keep His commandments, / For this is man's all."[29]

You see, what Ringer, Dyer, McWilliams, and others miss is that there is only one true, lasting source of happiness in life: God. As John Piper so clearly puts it in *Desiring God,* "The deepest and most enduring happiness is found only in God."[30] Making our happiness more important than God, or trying to find true happiness in something other than God, is a mistake that makes our lives miserable and unhappy.

If you are looking for something more stable than happiness, the Bible would steer you in the direction of contentment, which can be ours at all times regardless of our circumstances. Listen to the apostle Paul describe this in his own life: "Not that I speak in regard to need, for I have learned in whatever state I am, to be content."[31] This is coming from a man who experienced shipwreck, imprisonment, and beatings.

What does it take to be "content no matter what your circumstances are"? The right perspective—God's perspective. Paul understood that life is fleeting, that serving God is the name of the game, that God is more powerful than anything that came up against him, and that heaven was waiting on him at the end of his life. Those core truths, I believe, set Paul free from worry, enabling him to be content regardless of how good or bad things were at the moment. Having God's perspective on life provided Paul with contentment in spite of his trials.

If you want a better goal in life than being happy all the time, the Bible would offer the goal of becoming mature. The aim of the Christian life is to come to "the measure of the stature of the fullness of Christ."[32] Becoming like Christ—loving, gracious, truthful, self-controlled, transparent, forgiving—is a lifetime process that is never finished, but it is the only right goal.

If forewarned is forearmed, let me forearm you by suggesting that the goal of becoming mature actually insures that we will be unhappy at times. Part of becoming mature in Christ and "attaining to the whole measure" of who He is involves becoming a servant. Mature, Christlike people are willing to set aside their own happiness for the well-being of others. Christ did that when He died on the cross for our benefit. We are to take up our cross in the same way each day.

That may mean listening to someone talk about something painful in his life when we would rather watch television or read the paper. It may mean taking someone across town because her car died when we had planned to use the evening to play tennis. It may mean giving someone money for food when we had planned to spend that money on a new outfit. It may actually mean dying for the cause of Christ, as many throughout the centuries have done. Whatever specific form it may take, becoming more like Christ often means choosing that which is more painful and which temporarily produces unhappiness!

Let me remind you of a statement in the Bible that referred to Christ Himself: Christ was "a Man of sorrows and acquainted with grief."[33] You would think that if anyone would be constantly happy in life, it would have been a person who lived life perfectly. Yet, that is not the case. Christ was not constantly happy; He was, in fact, often unhappy. Yet, Christ was the most emotionally and spiritually healthy person ever to walk the planet.

The Bible isn't antihappiness; it just doesn't want our personal happiness to become our god. It encourages us to develop a godly perspective so that we will be content no matter what happens to us, and it challenges us to be more focused on becoming mature in Christ than on being happy. These are far superior aims and actually enhance our chances of being happy at times.

Ultimately, the Bible is trying to help us understand that true happiness can only be found in an intimate relationship with God. Blaise Pascal stated it so beautifully when he said:

> There was once in man a true happiness of which now remain to him only the dark and empty trace, which he in vain tries to fill from all his surroundings, seeking from things absent the help he does not find in things present. But these are all inadequate, because the infinite abyss can only be filled by an infinite and immutable object, that is to say, only by God himself.[34]

How does an intimate relationship with God bring us happiness? There are a number of ways, but let me mention two. First, God's love for us is something we come to understand more deeply as we get to know Him better, and there are few things that result in being happy like knowing you are unconditionally loved. Victor Hugo, in *Les Miserables,* put it this way: "The supreme happiness of life is the conviction that we are loved."[35] Second, an intimate relationship with God helps us see more clearly why we are here on earth, and this sense of purpose is vital for happiness. George Bernard Shaw, in *Man and Superman,* stated: "This is true joy in life, the being used for a purpose recognized by yourself as a mighty one; the being thoroughly worn out before you are thrown on the scrap heap; the being a force of nature instead of a feverish selfish little clod of ailments and grievances complaining that the world will not devote itself to making you happy."[36]

With all of his achievements, wisdom, wealth, power, and pleasures, Solomon came to a rather startling conclusion, which seems to fly in the face of all that we are told. While some self-help authors suggest that pleasure is the name of the game and that happiness is the ultimate goal in life, Solomon said those ways of thinking are the fastest path to a meaningless, unhappy, despair-filled life.

Wanting to be happy is a normal and good thing. Demanding that we be happy all the time and making happiness the central focus of our lives is pathological. In this light, the words of Blaise Pascal are well worth remembering:

> There are only three kinds of persons: those who serve God, having found Him; others who are occupied in seeking Him, not having found Him; while the remainder live without seeking Him, and without having found Him. The first are reasonable and happy, the last are foolish and unhappy; those between are unhappy and unreasonable.[37]

I encourage you to find God if you have not, and to serve Him if you have. Then, and only then, will you be truly happy.

CHAPTER 10

Pop psychology myth #10:

GOD CAN BE ANYTHING YOU WANT HIM TO BE

S mall groups have become a powerful force in our society. Millions of people are involved in small groups for all kinds of problems—everything from alcohol and drug addictions to "codependency" to overeating to shopping to sex to (I guess) small groups for small group addictions. You name it, and there is a small group for it.

Robert Wuthnow, Ph.D., is a professor of sociology at Princeton University and the director of Princeton's Center for the Study of American Religion. With the aid of the Lilly Endowment and the George H. Gallup International Institute, Dr. Wuthnow conducted a three-year national research project on small groups and spirituality.

According to Wuthnow, one out of every four Americans belongs to a small group, such as a Sunday school class, Bible-study group, political or civic group, twelve-step group, sports or hobby group, or singles group. Many of those who participate in these small groups swear by them, claiming they found close friends, overcame addictions, received emotional support, learned to forgive others, and grew spiritually. Yet, all is not well with the small group movement. Wuthnow discovered some unsettling facts about them. He writes:

> Yet the kind of community small groups create is quite different from the communities in which people lived in the past. These communities are more fluid and more concerned with the emotional states of the individual. Some small groups merely provide occasions for individuals to focus on themselves in the presence of others. What's more, the social contract binding members together asserts only the weakest of obligations. Come if you have time. Talk if you feel like it. Respect everyone's opinion. Never criticize. Leave quietly if you become dissatisfied. Families would never survive by following these operating norms. Close-knit communities in the past did not, either.[1]

Wuthnow goes on to make an even more important observation about small groups, this one related to how they impact the way we think of the sacred. He states:

> A majority of small-group members say they joined because they wanted to deepen their faith and that their sense of the sacred has been profoundly influenced by their participation. But small groups are not simply drawing people back to the God of their fathers and mothers. They are dramatically changing the way God is understood. God is now less of an external authority and more of an internal presence. The sacred becomes more personal, but, in the process, also becomes more manageable, more serviceable in meeting individual needs, and more a feature of the group process itself.[2]

Related to the focus of this chapter, Dr. Wuthnow makes one final observation that I want you to consider. He says:

> The deity of small groups is a God of love, comfort, order, and security. Gone is the God of judgment, wrath, justice, mystery, and punishment. Gone are concerns about the forces of evil. Missing from most groups, even, is a distinct interest in heaven and hell, except for the small heavens and hells that people experience in their everyday lives.[3]

In the original twelve steps program and the small groups based on them, you will find one of the worst, most destructive myths of all: the idea that God is whoever we understand or want Him to be. Physician William Playfair, in his book, *The Useful Lie,* sounds the alarm on this:

> These statements ["We came to believe that a Power greater than ourselves could restore us to sanity" and "We made a decision to turn our lives over to the care of God as we understood Him"] are especially disturbing because they allow and even encourage an addict to view God as a mere concept conformable to the addict's every wish. You can create a God of any sort you want. You can perceive him to be anything you think he is, or ought to be. You can call him anything or anyone you prefer—the choices are practically unlimited. Almost anything goes when it comes to the God of the Twelve Stepdom.[4]

The "God can be anything you want him to be" myth isn't limited to Alcoholics Anonymous only. The twelve steps and this "fuzzy" God permeate much of the recovery and self-help literature. As Wendy Kaminer notes in her book, *I'm Dysfunctional, You're Dysfunctional,* the concept of a higher power offered in many self-help books allows each of us to "submit to his or her own image of God."[5]

Let's take a look at the idea that God can be anything you want. How would you like people to interact with you based on who they view you to be when their view is based on only a small slice of who you really are? Let's say you have a lot of nice qualities but one of your not-so-nice qualities is that you are temperamental. How would it feel if someone saw you only as a temperamental person and interacted with you along those lines? It wouldn't feel good, would it? And you wouldn't feel that the person was really relating to you as a whole person.

The flip side of that problem would be equally uncomfortable. What if someone took just one of your positive qualities and treated you as if that were the whole you? Let's say, for example, that you are a very generous person. Think about how you would feel if that is the only way someone sees you and if that person responded to you this way all the time. Wouldn't you feel that the person who sees you as only having this one good trait isn't really seeing you for who you are and that you couldn't really have a genuine relationship with that person?

I wonder if this isn't what entertainment and sports celebrities feel most of the time. They are often revered because of some talent or quality they have, yet that talent or quality isn't who they are as a whole person. No wonder some begin to feel somewhat schizophrenic after a while. They are worshiped by the fans because they can act, sing, or whatever, yet who they really are as whole people is being ignored.

Now, let's put God into the picture. I wonder if

He doesn't feel the same way. I wonder if God isn't a little bit bothered when any of His attributes are selectively used to represent Him as a whole being. God deeply desires that we get to know Him intimately for who He really is. Reducing God to "this" or "that" keeps us from ever getting to know who He really is.

God is not reducible. You cannot take any of God's attributes and allow them to represent all of who He is without losing Him in the process. On a pop quiz, God is (D), all of the above, not A, B, or C.

I grew up in churches where various Sunday school teachers and pastors took certain attributes of God and taught them to me without including other attributes. I was taught a view of God that focused on His anger, wrath, and judgment. I don't think they meant any harm by it, but it did harm me just the same.

This angry, wrathful, and judgmental God scared the starch out of me. I don't remember feeling much like moving toward God as a I grew up. Instead, I often felt like running from Him. Even after I turned my life over to Christ when I was eleven or so, the "God" in my mind scared me. I saw God as carrying a proverbial "big stick," which He was delighted to use against me whenever I messed up.

I'm sure I was taught things about God other than just His "negative" traits. I do remember being taught, for example, that "Jesus loves the little children, all the children of the world." That comforted me. But, I don't remember being taught about that God often. As my sinfulness became more real to me, the teachings about God turning people into pillars of salt and destroying whole cities because of their wickedness came to the forefront of my mind, not His love and mercy. "Hellfire and brimstone" were more associated with God than were little children sitting in His lap.

I now look back and realize that I never *really* knew God during those times even though I did turn my life over to Him. I don't think I am alone in having experienced that.

Let me share with you some "versions" of God that are either inaccurate or contain only some small particle of truth about who God is:

- The "Big Stick" God: This is the god who hates the sin *and* the sinner and likes nothing more than to beat people on the head and condemn them.
- The "Absent Father" God: The god who doesn't care about his children's physical, emotional, and spiritual needs because he is too caught up in his own little world.
- The "Santa Claus" God: This is the god who is supposed to give you your every wish, want, and desire, especially if you have been a good person.

- The "User" God: The god who just wants to take, take, take from you and wants to give nothing back.
- The "Gooey" God: This is the god who has nothing but the warmest, gooiest feelings toward you, no matter what you have done.
- The "Play Favorites" God: This is the god who really does love some people more than others because they are smarter, prettier, more talented, or nicer.
- The "I'm Too Busy" God: This is the god who has so much stuff on his "To Do" list he doesn't have enough time for your puny concerns.
- The "Bailout" God: The god who rescues you from every mess you get yourself into, rather than allowing you to learn and mature by going through them.
- The "I Don't Know What I'm Doing" God: This is the god who hasn't the foggiest idea what he is doing and sits with a befuddled look on his face as the world goes in the wrong direction.
- The "Laughing" God: The god that thinks everything is one big joke. Nothing is a serious matter to this god.
- The "Wimp" God: This is the god who can't handle your real feelings or hear about your sins. He isn't strong enough to cope with tough issues or the fact that we might be angry or upset with him.

- The "Nerd" God. The god who is out of touch with what is going on in today's world. He is behind the times and doesn't really understand the complexities of living in today's world.

These are just a few of the distorted ways people think about God. Viewing God in any of these ways is destructive to your life. When self-help books teach you that God can be anything you understand him to be, they are giving you permission to create gods like these. The bottom line is that God is who He is, not who we want Him to be! We don't have the right or privilege to make God into something of our own creation, and it prohibits a close relationship with Him when we do.

So, who is God? How are we to view Him? These are extremely important questions, perhaps the most important you will ever ask. Let me take a shot at answering them.

. . . .

The God of the Bible

I am going to attempt to answer the question "Who is God?" even though I know full well that the most brilliant people on the planet could spend the rest of their lives trying to answer that question and not get close. God is infinite, and a finite mind simply cannot fully understand Him. As much as I believe God wants to be known by us and has done a great deal to make Himself known to us, He is incomprehensible. There are things we can know about God, yet there will always be aspects of Him that will be hidden from us. "The secret things belong to the LORD our God, but those things which are revealed belong to us and to our children forever. . . ."[6]

With it understood that "the finite cannot grasp the infinite," allow me to share with you how God describes Himself in the Bible.

God is eternal.[7] God never came into existence, because He is endlessly self-existent. R. C. Sproul, in *Essentials of the Christian Faith,* puts it this way: "Every effect must have a cause. This is true by definition. But God is not an effect. He has no beginning and therefore no antecedent cause. He is eternal. He always was or is. He has, within Himself, the power of being. He requires no assistance from outside sources to continue to exist."[8]

God is free.[9] No one directs God. He is independent of His creatures and is not obligated to us in any way. Whatever God does, He does because He chooses to do so. In this light, God can never be in our debt. That it why it is horribly misguided to think that God "owes" us anything for who we are or what we do.

God is unchanging.[10] God does not grow or develop. God is the same from one day to the next. This is an important characteristic of God, given the changing nature of society's values. We humans change as to what we say is right or wrong at a given time, but God does not change in terms of who He is or what He views as right or wrong.

God is infinite.[11] God knows no bounds or limits. God is not limited by space or time; He "transcends" them. He is not tied to the dimensions of life that we humans are.

God is holy.[12] This shows us two different aspects of God. First, it means that God is profoundly different from us. There is nothing and no one like Him. This uniqueness of God makes Him worthy of our reverence and adoration. Second, it means that God is perfectly pure, in that He always does what is right.

God is love.[13] God willfully and actively seeks the highest good for His creation. We say we "love" things such as ice cream, a sports team, or sunny days, but we don't really seek the highest good for these things. God's very nature is to seek the best for us all the time. Of course, the greatest expression of God's love is that He sent Christ to die for our sins.

God is omnipotent.[14] God is all-powerful and is able to do anything that is *consistent with His nature.* This means that while God is "Almighty" He cannot lie,[15] be tempted to sin,[16] or deny His own nature.[17] God's power is a source of great comfort for believers in two main ways. First, God's power is available to us in daily living as we face difficulties that are bigger than our own power to solve them.[18] Second, there is nothing that is powerful enough to stop God from doing what He says He is going to do.[19]

God is omnipresent.[20] This means both that God is present everywhere at all times and that His whole being is there (not some "part" of God). Since God is omnipresent, we don't have to go to a certain place at a certain time to be in His presence. We are in God's presence when we step into the spiritual dimension of life, something we can do anytime. R. C. Sproul, in *Essential Truths of the Christian Faith,* describes it this way:

> When we speak of God's omnipresence we usually mean that His presence is in all places. There is no place where God is not. Yet, as spirit, God does not occupy any place, in the sense that physical objects occupy space. He has no physical qualities that can occupy space. The key to understanding this paradox is to think in terms of another dimension. The barrier between God and us is not a barrier of space or time. To meet God, there is not a "where" to go to or a "when" to occur. To be in the immediate presence of God is to step into another dimension.[21]

God is omniscient.[22] God knows everything. He is a "know-it-all" in the best sense of the term. A. W. Tozier, in his book, *The Knowledge of the Holy,* describes God's omniscience much better than I can:

God knows instantly and effortlessly all matter and all matters, all mind and every mind, all spirit and all spirits, all being and every being, all creaturehood and all creatures, every plurality and all pluralities, all law and every law, all relations, all causes, all thoughts, all mysteries, all enigmas, all feelings, all desires, every unuttered secret, all thrones and dominions, all personalities, all things visible and invisible in heaven and in earth, motion, space, time, life, death, good, evil, heaven, and hell.

Because God knows all things perfectly, He knows no thing better than any other thing, but all things equally well. He never discovers anything, He is never surprised, never amazed. He never wonders about anything nor (except when drawing man out for their own good) does He seek information or ask questions.[23]

God is truth.[24] God and His revelation are completely reliable; He has revealed himself as He really is. Whatever God says is trustworthy because He cannot lie. If you find a promise in Scripture, you can depend on it because God will never break it or fail to fulfill it. The Bible is inerrantly true because God, its Author, is Truth.

God is merciful.[25] God sometimes gives less punishment to wrongdoers than they deserve and more reward to "rightdoers" than they deserve. However, God does not have to be merciful, nor does He have to justify His mercy.

God is good.[26] Everything God does is good. He doesn't have a mean bone in His spirit. Not only is God Himself good, He is the source of all good things.[27] On top of both being good and offering us good things, God promises to make "all things work together for good to those who love God."[28] So no matter how bad something may be at the moment, God will ultimately make good come out of it for believers.

When I look through this incredible list of God's attributes, I am awestruck. Any one quality by itself would be amazing, yet God possesses them all. Sadly, many Christians struggle with worry, fear, depression, and other emotional problems, partly because they don't really believe that God is all these things. Faith, in part, means accepting that what God says about Himself is true even if appearances are to the contrary. We can have confidence that God is in control of everything, only does things for our good, is just, and so on, even if everything looks out of control, bad, unfair, and so on. Not to believe what God says about Himself in the Bible is to call Him a liar.

Can you imagine possessing even one characteristic of God's? Can you imagine, for example, being all-knowing? Merciful? Good? If you and I had just one of God's characteristics in its fullness, we would be incredible people by human standards. When you think about it, aren't the people we admire usually the ones who have some high degree of some of these characteristics? God has them *all* in their fullness, yet do we admire Him as much?

Compare the characteristics of God listed in this chapter with how you hear God talked about in day-to-day conversation. People frequently say things like "God really let me down" or "I'm really angry with God" or "God hates me" or "God doesn't really care about me." These statements represent a shallow understanding of God. God *never* lets His people down. We may not like what God is doing or how He is doing it, but God never fails to do what is best for us.

God must be worshiped in "spirit and truth" if He is to be worshiped properly. We worship God "in spirit" because He is spirit. We worship God "in truth" because to worship Him for anything less than what He is, is to worship an idol of our own creation and, thus, a lie. Pop psychology books that encourage you to worship God "as you understand Him" are horribly misguided. God will not be worshiped "as you understand Him." God will only be worshiped as He is!

CONCLUSION

SELF-HELP
OR
GOD-HELP?

Things are worse in our country today than they were half a century ago. There are a number of reasons for this, but I believe one of the main reasons is that we have become a psychological society that worships self rather than a moral society that worships God. Martin Gross, in his book, *The Psychological Society,* put it this way:

> As the Protestant ethic has weakened in Western society, the confused citizen has turned to the only alternative he knows: the psychological expert who claims there is a new scientific standard of behavior to replace fading traditions. . . . Mouthing the holy

name of science, the psychological expert claims to know all. This new truth is fed to us continuously from birth to the grave.[1]

Those who write pop psychology books appear to have good intentions. They really do seem to want to help us overcome painful emotional problems and enjoy fulfilling lives. But the fact that they want to help us doesn't mean they really know how; their good intentions oftentimes result in doing us more harm than good. Their hearts are in the right place, it's just that their heads seem to be somewhere else. If, as author John Gray suggests, "men are from Mars, women are from Venus," far too many pop psychology authors seem, judging by what they teach, to be from a different solar system altogether.

One of the main perceptions I walked away with after reading seventy-five self-help books in preparation for writing this book is that many of these authors are more concerned with making us feel happy than with teaching us how to be mature. The pricetag for becoming a truly mature adult is that we will frequently be called upon to do things that are painful, things that will make us feel unhappy for a while. Too many pop psychology books seem afraid to tell us this truth, probably because the "positive stuff" sells books. Pop psychology books often tell us what our "itching ears"[2] want to hear in an effort to create immediate relief; yet, in the long run, we are worse off.

Another perception I came away with is that many self-help books are more concerned with whether or not a concept or idea makes us feel good than with whether or not it is true. Pop psychology books often seem to operate under the assumption that if a teaching makes us feel better, it must be true. I hope you have realized that there are a lot of ideas that make us feel good that are simply untrue. Truth is not necessarily associated with feeling good.

A third perception is that many pop psychology books seem to suggest you can master a set of techniques and find health and happiness. "Do A, B, and C, and your life will be fantastic." As Wendy Kaminer put it in her book, *I'm Dysfunctional, You're Dysfunctional,* "What sells self-help books, tapes, and workshops is the willingness to believe that there are experts who can help us achieve the good life, however it is defined at the moment; existential problems are reduced to merely technical ones, which can be solved by expert techniques."[3]

I don't believe there are any magic formulas or techniques for mastering life; life is too difficult, complex, and mysterious to be mastered. I do believe there are certain tasks, permanent "homework assignments," if you will, that we need to work on day by day; the better we get at them, the better our lives will be. Let me share five of them with you.

First, we need to work each day on the task of taking responsibility. Ever since Adam and Eve sinned in the Garden of Eden and blamed something outside themselves for the sin, finger-pointing has been common practice in the world. It is much more common to hear someone say, "He made me mad" or "She is driving me crazy" than it is to hear someone have the courage to say, "I chose to become angry" or "I am choosing to drive myself nuts." Everything seems to be someone else's fault. We must stop blaming other people for the things that are wrong with us, and we must take responsibility each day for our thoughts, feelings, and actions if our lives are to ever get any better.

Second, we need to work hard each day on the task of keeping first things first. Or, as Pastor Peter Lord of Park Avenue Baptist Church in Titusville, Florida, puts it, "The main thing is to keep the main thing the main thing." We often have our priorities all backwards. We allow relatively unimportant things, like watching television or lowering our golf score or developing "buns of steel," to take precedence over being intimate with God and loved ones, serving people in need, raising our children properly, and doing meaningful work. We mismanage our time, allowing the most important things in life to be squeezed out by what seems to be the most urgent. The main things in life must be given priority over the minor things in life.

Third, we must work daily on the task of reigning in our need for pleasure. We seem to have become a country that operates on the notion, "If it feels good, do it." Yet, our need to feel good at the moment with little concern for how it will impact us and others down the road is destroying us. For example, young people are having sex earlier and more often, and far too many of them are becoming parents when they are clearly not equipped for the job. Also, we abuse charge cards like there is no tomorrow, getting everything we want *now!* whether we have the money for it or not. Our motto these days unfortunately seems to be "He who dies with the most toys wins!" We must learn to say no to ourselves when necessary and postpone pleasure until its proper time.

Fourth, we need to spend time each day renewing our minds with the truth. All of us suffer from beliefs that are irrational, erroneous, unrealistic, and misguided. These beliefs must be replaced with the truth if we are ever to enjoy true emotional well-being and become mature people. The computer expression, "Garbage in, garbage out," applies to what we tell ourselves mentally each day. We must stop believing "garbage" and start believing the truth. As the apostle Paul told the Christians in the church at Ephesus, "That we should no longer be children, tossed to and fro and carried about with every wind of doctrine, by the trickery of men, in the cunning craftiness of deceitful plotting."[4] Each day we must attack the lies we believe with biblical truth in the most direct and aggressive way possible so that the truth can be allowed to set us free.

Fifth, and most important, we must stop playing around with "spirituality" and start spending time each day getting to know the one true God of the universe better. People seem to be seeking deeper spiritual lives these days, but so many of them have gone off in directions that actually take them away from God. The New Age movement offers everything from astral projection to yoga to rebirthing to inner guides to Zen. By pursuing spirituality through these means, they miss the only real God in the Universe. We must return to the God of the Bible if authentic spiritual lives are to be ours.

The teachings of the Bible offer better "psychology" than what psychology offers. While there are areas of overlap between what the Bible teaches and what pop psychology teaches (loving your neighbor, forgiving those who have hurt you, living more fully in the here and now, becoming more authentic) pop psychology is just not up to the task of helping people lead whole lives. The Bible, however, offers a deeper picture of who we really are, the true meaning and purpose of our lives, what maturity really is and how to move toward it, what to do about sin and guilt, what genuine love and intimacy are all about, and where we are headed after we die. Psychology never has offered—and never will—the depth of insight and understanding that we need in order to live life fully.

The danger in most pop psychology books is that they offer just enough truth to make us think that all of what they teach is true and trustworthy. On the following pages (162–163) you can see the pop psychology myths I have examined side by side with the corresponding biblical truths. Take one more look at how they stack up against each other. Ask yourself which view is more likely to take you in the direction of emotional health and spiritual maturity. Most important, ask yourself which of the two you actually believe and practice each day.

We all make a grave error if we think that just *knowing* the truth is sufficient for becoming healthy, mature people. We must *experience* and *live* the truth if it is to become real and effective to us. That is what James is talking about when he states, "But be doers of the word, and not hearers only, deceiving yourselves."[5] Or, as James Boice so aptly stated in his book, *Foundations of the Christian Faith,* "We must not assume that we will be able fully to understand any passage of Scripture unless we are willing to be changed by it."[6]

Unfortunately, my application of truth is often miles behind my knowledge of it. Many of those in the people-helping field seem to struggle with the same problem. Most of us know a fair amount about human dynamics and personal growth, but many of us are not applying very much of what we know. A lot of knowledge can help make a person pretty arrogant

Pop Psychology Myth	Biblical Truth
1. People are basically good.	1. People are neither neutral nor good but sinful by nature. Our natural bent is to miss the moral mark of living how God wants us to live.
2. You need more self-esteem and self-worth.	2. Self-esteem, being tied to performance, should not always be high because our performances in life aren't always high. We have worth because God created us in His image.
3. You can't love others until you love yourself.	3. All of us love ourselves already, in that we naturally look out for our own best interests. We can love others even if we don't love ourselves because true love is willful action aimed at helping someone mature. This kind of love can be offered to others no matter how we feel about ourselves.
4. You shouldn't judge anyone.	4. We are to first put our own thoughts and actions under God's scrutiny before we judge others. Doing so creates humility and leads to judgments about others that will be more accurate as well as motivated by grace and compassion.
5. All guilt is bad.	5. We all sin (fall short of the moral mark), and we need to experience guilt when we do. There is a type of guilt (worldly) that is bad; it doesn't

Pop Psychology Myth	Biblical Truth
	result in true change. Yet, there is a type of guilt (godly sorrow) that comes from God that results in genuine change and is good for us.
6. You need to think positively.	6. First and foremost, we are to think the truth. Whether a thought is positive or negative is unimportant.
7. Staying "in love" is the key to a great relationship.	7. Loving someone by committing yourself to willfully act in his or her best interest is the key to a great relationship. Being "in love" with someone comes and goes; it is not the key to a great relationship.
8. You have unlimited power and potential.	8. You have power and potential in life that is limited by your gifts, abilities, and, to a certain degree, circumstances. You can't achieve anything you want in life, but you can make important contributions, and you need to make sure you don't settle for contributing less than you are capable of.
9. Your happiness is the most important thing in life.	9. Becoming mature in Christ is the most important thing in life, even if it means being unhappy at times.
10. God can be anything you want Him to be.	10. God must be seen for who He really is. If you make God into who you want Him to be, you are not actually involved with the one true God.

if that knowledge isn't applied. A friend and colleague of mine, Dr. Sandy Wilson, reminds all of us highly educated people helpers of this when she says that we need to remember that "Ph.D." doesn't stand for "People Helping Deity."

We all want and need help as we go through life. The issue isn't "Do we need help?" but "Where are we going to go for the help that we need?"

. . . .

God Is Our Help

My son, Matt, when he was younger, was a huge "Ghostbusters" fan. He and his best buddy down the street, Nicholas, got everything they could lay their hands on that had anything to do with Ghostbusters. They had Ghostbusters uniforms, backpacks, and ray guns. Matt also had the soundtrack from the movie. If I heard the Ghostbusters' theme once, I heard it a million times back then. You may remember that the theme song raised the question, "Who ya gonna call?" when there is "something strange in the neighbor-hood." You call the Ghostbusters, of course, and they will save you from any ghost, ghoul, or goblin that is haunting you.

Long before the Ghostbusters asked, "Who ya gonna call?" someone else did. The Psalmist put it this way: "I will lift up my eyes to the hills—from whence comes my help?"[7] When we are in need, when life has collapsed all around us and even on top of us, when everything seems to be going wrong and there appear to be no solutions in sight, where will our help come from?

A frequent answer to that question these days seems to be "myself." We live in an age in which each of us is supposed to look out for Number One—win through intimidation, wake up the giant within, be our own best friend, and pull our own strings. In other words, you can't depend on anyone else but yourself. Those who write the pop psychology books that suggest such things never really say why you and I are any more trustworthy than anyone else as the source of help in our lives. Frankly, if I turn to myself as *the* source of help in my life, I am just as likely to mess things up as anyone else I might turn to.

Where will our help come from? Another frequent answer to that question is "experts." We put so much trust in the psychological experts of our day. Somehow, we have come to see them as the ones "in the know" when, in spite of what they do know, there is a lot they are wrong on and a great deal they are simply ignorant about. That, obviously, includes me. None of us so-called experts are infallible, so there isn't a single counselor, self-help book, or pop psychology audiotape on the planet that you can put your complete trust in. I personally think we ought to stop using the term "expert" to describe any human being because of the arrogance of such a title and the blind faith it tends to engender. Instead, I would suggest a term like "apprentice" because we are always learning, no matter how much we may know.

So, "who ya gonna call" when you need help? The Psalmist not only raises the question, he answers it: "My help comes from the Lord, who made heaven and earth."[8] Pretty simple and straightforward, isn't it? Our help, first and foremost, comes from God. Sadly, it seems like most of us turn to Him as a last resort. Yet, to say that God is our true source of help in life doesn't say *how* He helps us, does it? Let me take a crack at answering that question.

God helps us in a number of important ways. First, He took care of our most pressing need for help when He offered up His Son, Jesus Christ, as an atonement for our sins. You've heard that a million times before, I know, but I just wanted to remind you that this was God's greatest, most sacrificial effort to help us. You and I owed a spiritual debt we could not pay, and God paid it with the blood of His only Son. Had He not offered us help in this way, all of us would be doomed to spend eternity in hell.

In addition to helping us by forgiving our sins through faith in Christ, God helps us through His Holy Spirit. I don't pretend to know even one-tenth of all that the Holy Spirit does on our behalf, but I do know He offers us help in a number of ways. The Holy Spirit helps us understand truth (John 16:13), convicts us of sin (John 16:8), internally testifies to us that we are God's children (Romans 8:16), illuminates biblical truth (1 Corinthians 2:9–11), comforts us (John 14:16), makes intercession on our behalf with God the Father and helps us find strength when we are weak (Romans 8:26–27), and helps us become mature (2 Corinthians 3:17–18). Think about these and you will come to appreciate the tremendous source of help that the Holy Spirit is.

Obviously, another way God helps us is by providing truth in the form of His Word, the Bible. We don't have to wonder what the most important truths in life are because God divinely inspired mortal man to write them down for our enlightenment and application. In a world where so much nonsense is passed off as wisdom, we don't have to be confused or in the dark about what truth is. If people need the truth to be set free, the Bible is God's way of giving us the truths we must believe for true freedom in life.

"All Scripture is given by inspiration of God, and is profitable for doctrine, for reproof, for correction, for instruction in righteousness, that the man of God may be complete, thoroughly equipped for every good work."[9] I don't think you will find that claim accurately fitting any other book you might read. We have all kinds of books by human authors, and these books reflect the fact that they are written by humans: they contain errors in them. When a book is "given by inspiration of God," you can trust what it says completely and find answers in it that you can base your life on.

There is yet another way that God helps us, and that is through relationships with other people, especially other Christians. We all need intimate relationships with people in order to be healthy and mature, and God works through our relationships with others to meet our needs for support, encouragement, comfort, and challenge. The Greek word in the Bible for the relationship element among believers is *koinonia,* and it is a rich term indeed. Koinonia refers to an extremely deep commitment that Christians are supposed to have to one another related to sharing their common life in Christ. It is something that God commands us to do and is not to be taken lightly. The apostle Paul captures true koinonia best in some of his statements to the Christians in Rome and Galatia. Here are just a few:

- "Be kindly affectionate to one another with brotherly love, in honor giving preference to one another."[10]
- "[Distribute] to the needs of the saints, given to hospitality."[11]
- "Rejoice with those who rejoice, and weep with those who weep."[12]
- "Be of the same mind toward one another. Do not set your mind on high things, but associate with the humble. Do not be wise in your own opinion."[13]

- "If it is possible, as much as depends on you, live peaceably with all men."[14]
- "Therefore, as we have opportunity, let us do good to all, especially to those who are of the household of faith."[15]

I think you can tell from just this small sampling of verses that Christians are to take relationships with one another very seriously. The emphasis here is clearly on community, not Lone Rangerism. Sadly, too many churches and Christian groups don't practice what Paul is talking about. Because the depth of fellowship we are supposed to have with Christ and with one another as Christians oftentimes isn't there, the non-Christian world isn't attracted to what we have. True koinonia, when it is lived out with other Christians, is not only one of the primary ways God ministers His grace to us, but is also how He hopes to attract others into His family.

One final way that God helps us is through giving each Christian at least one "spiritual gift." These gifts are given to us so that we can effectively minister to the needs of other Christians. They include the gifts of service, teaching, mercy, encouragement, and leadership. Not only are we helped when other Christians use their spiritual gifts to minister to us, but I believe God gives each of us at least one spiritual gift as His way of telling us we have something very valuable to offer in return.

The ultimate question to ask yourself is "Will I accept the help that I am offered?" God, as our helper, has promised to meet all of our needs "according to His riches in glory by Christ Jesus."[16] That is quite a promise. God isn't going to meet just some of our needs; He is going to meet them all. That is the kind of helper He is. But, will we accept the help that He offers?

I was coming out of an electronics store once when two women in a car pulled up and asked me for directions. I knew where they wanted to go and how to get them there, so I proceeded to give them very clear directions. They listened, shook their heads as if they understood, and drove off. I stood there for a minute watching them as they were about to exit the parking lot. The first instruction I gave them was to turn right. Guess what they did? Yep, they turned left. I stood there shaking my head, thinking, "What is wrong with those two? How could I have been any clearer? Now they are going to end up who knows where!"

I wonder if God doesn't feel that way toward us at times. He gives us the clearest directions possible on how to arrive at the destination called "An Abundant Life." He carefully explains the different decisions we will face and what the best choice is. He tries to route us on the best roads available so that we avoid roads full of unnecessary potholes and hazards. We listen (sometimes), nod our heads (as if we understand), and proceed to turn left when He tells us to turn right. We get lost and experience a great deal of turmoil, and then we have the nerve to rail against God for our being in the mess we are in.

My favorite verse in all of the Bible reads: "For I know the thoughts that I think toward you, says the LORD, thoughts of peace and not of evil, to give you a future and a hope."[17] Part of God's plan to help you involves steering you away from nonsense "lest anyone should deceive you with persuasive words."[18] Pop psychology books, in spite of the help they offer, have been and will continue to be a significant source of nonsense, and God knows the horrible damage they can do to your soul. His plan to help you involves steering you back to Himself and the truths in the Bible so that He can truly change your life for the better.

In closing, allow me to challenge you as the apostle Paul once challenged the Christians in the church at Colosse: "Beware lest anyone cheat you through philosophy and empty deceit, according to the tradition of men, according to the basic principles of the world, and not according to Christ."[19]

May God bless your efforts to meet this tremendously important challenge.

APPENDIX A

A BRIEF HISTORY
OF SELF-HELP
BOOKS IN
AMERICA

Dr. Steven Starker, in his book, *Oracle at the Supermarket: The American Preoccupation With Self-Help Books,* provides an excellent review of the history of self-help books. In this Appendix, I will borrow heavily from his work to give you a feel for the influential role self-help books have played in America. For a more in-depth and scholarly understanding of this topic, I highly recommend Dr. Starker's book.

Dr. Starker suggests that the roots of self-help literature in this country are found in the Puritans who settled the original colonies. The Puritans believed that God created the universe and that if they lived up to their obligations to God by doing good works He would live up to His obligations to them by helping them have successful lives. Bishop Bayly's *The Practice of Piety* (1611), Samuel Hardy's *Guide to Heaven* (1673), and Cotton Mather's *Bonifacius: Essays to Do Good* (1710) are examples of Puritan works that stressed the importance of hard work, dedication, and commitment that each individual needs to exhibit toward God in order to be successful.

Secular self-help books became more common in America by the eighteenth century. Benjamin Franklin wrote a number of books that emphasized personal effort and ambition in moving up the social hierarchy. In his book, *The Way to Wealth* (1757), he taught that living according to the virtues of humility, chastity, tranquility, cleanliness, moderation, justice, sincerity, resolution, order, silence, temperance, prudence, frugality, and industry was the way to personal prosperity. Franklin's *Poor Richard's Almanac* (1732–1757) is a well-known classic in which Franklin trumpeted these same themes. Many others wrote self-help books during the eighteenth century as well, helping to establish the self-help book as a source of much needed guidance on how to live life.

In the nineteenth century, there were significant social and economic changes taking place in America. Many felt quite alarmed by the moral decay they observed in the large cities. These conditions helped produce a great deal of literature on how to properly conduct one's life. In reacting to the immorality of the day, William McGuffey wrote self-improvement books for children during that time. His books were widely distributed, with more than 120 million copies of his *Eclectic Reader* being sold. McGuffey's readers told children that personal effort was the key in rising up in life and that traditional values (like those espoused by Benjamin Franklin) must be practiced in order to stop the country's moral decline. One McGuffey lesson encouraged children to never give up:

Try, Try Again
If you find your task is hard
Try, try again;
Time will bring you your reward,
Try, try again;
All that other folks can do,
Why, with patience, should not you?
Only keep this rule in view:
Try, try again.

In the late nineteenth and early twentieth centuries, many self-help authors focused on how to obtain financial wealth through the practice of certain virtues. Perhaps the most well-known of these authors was Horatio Alger. It is estimated that he wrote over one hundred books that sold approximately seventeen million copies. Alger's books had a "rags to riches" theme to them: If you practice honesty, prudence, frugality, and the other virtues, you will be a success. Alger, like many during that time, was concerned about how capitalism was changing people's lives and how certain individuals lacking in moral character were amassing great fortunes. His theme was that a good Christian life was the most important thing and that worldly success would be a by-product of that.

A different kind of self-help book began to appear in the early twentieth century. Based on a philosophy referred to as "New Thought" and tied to the writings of Ralph Waldo Emerson, these self-help books stressed the importance of the spiritual over the material while still focusing on worldly success. The thrust of many of these books was that God is some kind of a spiritual power or force and that all we have to do is use our minds to let Him know what our wishes are and He will provide. Bruce MacLelland's *Prosperity Through Thought Force* (1904), Elizabeth Towne's *Practical Methods for Self-Development* (1904), Orison Marden's *Peace, Power, and Plenty* (1909), and Napoleon Hill's *Think and Grow Rich* (1937) are examples of New Thought self-help books. The bottom line here was you just needed the right attitude and a prosperity mind set, and everything else would take care of itself. For example, Elizabeth Towne, in *Practical Methods for Self-Development,* wrote:

> The only thing that keeps us from taking plenty of money or air is fear. . . . We take in breath or money

by expanding. We force out air or money by contracting. The trouble with us is that we are afraid to expand. We try to bring our ideas and our wants all down to a smaller scale. We are afraid to take in big thoughts and ideas, lest we be disappointed. We are afraid to expect more than a couple of dollars or so a day. . . . Wake up. Expand. Take deep, full breaths of air, and your mind and purse expand in sympathy with your lungs. . . . Money is really as free as air. Take it in by knowing that it is yours.

New Thought not only focused on attaining financial success, but it also focused on the use of the mind to heal. Phineas Quimby is credited with starting the mind-cure tradition in America. Born in 1802, Quimby came to believe that all disease was a delusion, an error of the mind, and that the mind could heal any form of disease by simply overcoming the faulty thinking that made you think you had the disease in the first place. In other words, if you think you have a disease you are deceiving yourself and as soon as you see there is no such thing as disease you will be fine.

Phineas Quimby was followed by people like Reverend Warren Evans who wrote *The Mental Cure* (1869), Mary Baker Eddy, the founder of Christian Science, who wrote *Science and Health* (1885), and Henry Wood, author of *Ideal Suggestion through Mental Photography: A Restorative System for Home and Private Use* (1893). They agreed with Quimby that the power of the mind could bring about healing. Wood, for example, encouraged his readers to find a quiet corner, relax, breathe deeply, and meditate on statements like "There is no death" and "I am not body."

The Great Depression, the rise of psychology, and the baby boom each exerted a strong influence on the self-help books published in the 1900's. Harry Emerson Fosdick, a minister, attempted to integrate psychology with theology when his efforts at pastoral counseling seemed to be deficient in the face of the kinds of personal problems people experienced. His book, *On Being a Real Person* (1943), sold over 200,000 copies in one year. In 1946, Rabbi Joshua Liebman published *Peace of Mind,* also an attempt to integrate religion with psychology. By 1956, it had sold over a million copies. Dale Carnegie, writing mainly for business people, published *How to Win Friends and Influence People* in 1937. It sold 729,000 copies in its first year and has gone on to sell over six million copies. Carnegie's book taught that knowledge and technical ability alone were not enough and that being skillful with people was equally important. Dr. Benjamin Spock wrote *The Pocket Book of Baby and Child Care* in 1946, and it has since sold over thirty million copies.

Books on sexual behavior were also big best-sellers in America. Obviously, not only is the public interested in business success, personal growth, and how to raise kids, but it also wants to know how things should be in the bedroom. Sylvester Graham, in *A Lecture to Young Men, on Chastity* (1834), taught that sexual activity reduces your "life force" and that abstinence and diet could replenish it.

Other books on sex were popular as well. Mary Wood-Allen, M.D., wrote *Marriage: Its Duties and Privileges* (1901), and in that book told women that it was normal for them to have little or no sexual feeling and that a husband's sexual interest needed to be endured as a way of having children. The Kinsey report on *Sexual Behavior in the Human Male* (1948), not a self-help book per se, was purchased by many in hopes of finding personal help for sexual difficulties. It sold 225,000 copies in its first year. Eustace Chesser, M.D., wrote *Love Without Fear: How to Achieve Sex Happiness in Marriage* in 1947, and it has since sold millions of copies. Some of the more popular titles in recent years include: *Sex and the Single Girl* (1962), by Helen Gurley Brown, *Everything You Always Wanted to Know about Sex but Were Afraid to Ask* (1969) by David Reuben, *Open Marriage* (1972) by Nena and George O'Neill, and *The Joy of Sex* (1972) by Alex Comfort.

Self-help books on health and diet have been and continue to be hugely successful in our country. Hundreds of them have been written, and they have sold millions and millions of copies. Lulu Hunt Peters wrote *Diet and Health with Key to the Calories* in

1918. It made the best-seller list for five years and total sales are estimated to be over 800,000 copies. Victor Lindlahr wrote *You Are What You Eat* in 1940, and it has sold over 1.5 million copies. If Lindlahr is right and you are what you eat, I am in big trouble given what I wolf down everyday. *Live Longer, Look Younger,* written in 1950 by Gayelord Hauser, was a big best-seller. Hauser taught that "you need not be old at eighty, ninety" and that proper eating could nourish "your mind, heart, spirit, your total personality." Maybe that is what's wrong with my personality! *The Doctor's Quick Weight Loss Diet,* written by physician Irwin Stillman in 1967, has sold over five million copies, even though its critics said that following the diet could contribute to health problems. *Dr. Atkins' Diet Revolution,* released in 1972, was also a huge best-seller even though it was also criticized for being potentially dangerous. Other health and diet books that have been quite popular include *The Complete Scarsdale Medical Diet* (1978), *The Pritikin Program for Diet and Exercise* (1978), *Richard Simmons' Never-Say-Diet Book* (1981), *Jane Fonda's Workout Book* (1981), and *Stop the Insanity* (1993) by Susan Powter.

Recently, the trend in self-help books has been in two directions. One direction has been termed "selfist." Books that fall into this category hold up the "self" as supreme and encourage self-expression and self-actualization. "Do your own thing" and "get in touch with yourself" would be appropriate mottoes for many of these books. Maxwell Maltz's *Psycho-cybernetics* (1960), Eric Berne's *Games People Play* (1964), Thomas A. Harris's *I'm OK-You're OK* (1967), Mildred Newman and Bernard Berkowitz's *How to Be Your Own Best Friend* (1971), Wayne Dyer's *Your Erroneous Zones* (1976) and *Pulling Your Own Strings* (1978), Robert Ringer's *Looking Out for #1* (1977), and Melody Beattie's *Codependent No More* (1989) all fit into the category of "selfist" self-help books.

Another direction self-help books have taken recently is toward "pop theology." Two earlier works that set the stage for this were Fulton Sheen's *Peace of Soul* (1949) and Norman Vincent Peale's *The Power of Positive Thinking* (1952). Sheen argued in his book that man had become too self-centered and had been willing to settle for peace of mind rather than peace of soul. He believed that psychoanalysis could not really help people deal with guilt since it denied personal responsibility. The key to peace of soul was to return to God and live by an absolute ethical system. Dr. Peale's book, which has sold millions of copies, emphasized overcoming the "inferiority complex" by staying focused on one's strengths and visualizing God as a source of help. Peale taught that personal unhappiness is self-created for the most part, and he offered many practical solutions for practicing "happy thinking" so as to develop a "happiness habit." More recent contributions to the pop theology literature include Robert Shuller's *Self-Esteem, The New Reformation* (1982), Harold Kushner's *When Bad Things Happen to Good People* (1984), and Thomas Moore's *Care of the Soul* (1992).

I conclude with one final note from Dr. Starker's book. He conducted research to examine psychologists' attitudes toward self-help books. His findings were that psychologists frequently read self-help books, are quite positive in their assessment of them, and frequently prescribe them to their patients. Concerned by these findings, Dr. Starker writes:

> Self-help titles, by and large, are repositories of unproven, sometimes unprovable, advice on matters of considerable importance and complexity. That clinicians are willing to endorse and prescribe such works raises uncomfortable questions regarding professional practice and ethics, particularly for those advocating a scientist/practitioner model. Have many practitioners "sold out" their professional values, and abandoned their scientific standards, in favor of purveying "pop" psychology? Are they reading popularized works instead of the research literature? Are they adopting "pop" frameworks because mainstream theoretical approaches have been found, in some manner, unsatisfactory?

Dr. Starker acknowledges that definitive answers to these questions are not available, but the answer to them would seem to be "Yes." Self-help books do appear to have taken on a very important role in the practice of psychotherapy in spite of the fact that what these books teach is frequently unproven.

As you can see from this brief review, self-help books have been an important part of the American landscape ever since the country began. Literally hundreds of millions of these books have been sold over the centuries, and the influence they have exerted over people's lives is immeasurable.

APPENDIX B

THURMAN'S GUIDELINES FOR SELECTING A SELF-HELP BOOK

Before offering you guidelines for choosing a self-help book, I want to suggest that the process of deciding which books are worth your time and attention is like deciding who to marry: You can make some judgments based on externals, but the best decisions are made by spending time investigating what's on the inside. Keeping that in mind, here are my guidelines:

1. Do not buy a self-help book because it has a catchy title, an attractive cover, or makes incredible claims (like "perfect mental health in ten days" or "how to be happy all the time"). Catchy titles and attractive covers don't tell you anything about the quality of what is on the inside of the book, and a

book that makes grandiose claims is more likely to harm you than help you.

2. Avoid books that offer simplistic formulas for how to live life successfully. Life is too complex and people are too multidimensional for these to work. At the same time, make sure the books you read offer you specific help on how to apply what you are learning so that you "do not merely listen" but "do what it says" (James 1:22).

3. Check the author's credentials. Credentials certainly don't tell the whole story, but they are an important indication of how qualified the author is to write about a given topic.

4. Choose books that focus on a specific issue rather than those that try to tackle all of your problems at once. The more focused a book is on a particular issue, the more helpful it is likely to be.

5. Avoid self-help books that use a lot of psychobabble. Authors who don't write in plain English are usually revealing that they really don't know what they are talking about.

6. Avoid self-help books that focus on "self" at the expense of building intimate relationships with others and personal happiness at the expense of becoming mature. Books that make you and your happiness the center of the universe are poison to your soul and need to be avoided.

7. Check out the worldview of the author. All authors have one, and it significantly influences what

they say in their books. If an author does not believe in the God of the Bible, thinks that human beings are in control of everything, believes truth originates with human beings, holds that true meaning and purpose in life can be found apart from God, believes that morality is a relative thing, views human nature as good or neutral, and believes that people have little control or absolute control over their lives, what that author has to say is highly suspect and probably not worth your time.

The bottom line in evaluating a self-help book as far as I am concerned is this: Does it lead to "truth in the innermost being?" (Psalm 51:6). Truth is God's possession, truth sets people free, and truth must be what a self-help book is taking us toward. Self-help books that help us deeply understand and live the truth are taking us in the direction of God and in the direction of an abundant life. These books are worth our time and attention.

NOTES

INTRODUCTION: Pop Psychologists Say the Craziest Things

1. Torrey 1992, 131.
2. Watson 1928, 81–82.
3. Ibid., 84–85.
4. Passantino and Passantino 1995, 22.

CHAPTER 1: Pop Psychology Myth #1: People Are Basically Good

1. Beattie 1987, 122.
2. McWilliams 1991, 79.
3. Prager 1994, 1.
4. Ibid., 2.
5. Maslow 1968, 4.
6. Ibid., iv.
7. Colson 1993, 4–5.
8. Calvin 1986, 211.
9. Sproul 1992, 146.
10. Romans 3:23.
11. Galatians 5:19–21.
12. Menninger 1973, 13.
13. Romans 3:10–12.

CHAPTER 2: Pop Psychology Myth #2: You Need More Self-Esteem and Self-Worth

1. McKay and Fanning 1987, 50.
2. Ibid., 185.
3. Ibid., 186.
4. Ibid., 186.
5. Ibid., 186.
6. Ibid., 274.

7. Genesis 1:27.
8. Genesis 1:31.
9. Psalm 8:5–6.
10. Psalm 139:14.

CHAPTER 3: Pop Psychology Myth #3:
You Can't Love Others until You Love Yourself

1. McWilliams 1995, v–ix.
2. Ibid., xvii.
3. Beattie 1987, 126–27.
4. Schwartz 1982, 232.
5. Ibid., 233.
6. Ibid., 233.
7. Narramore 1978, 22.
8. Trobisch 1976, 33.
9. Captain 1984.
10. Matthew 22:36–39.
11. Vine 1985, 382.
12. Brownback 1982, 56.
13. Ephesians 5:29.
14. 2 Timothy 3:1–5.
15. Vitz 1977.
16. Proverbs 3:34.
17. Ephesians 4:2.
18. Philippians 2:3.
19. Matthew 16:24.
20. 1 John 4:7–12.

CHAPTER 4: Pop Psychology Myth #4:
You Shouldn't Judge Anyone

1. McKay and Fanning 1987, 293.
2. Ibid., 293.
3. Ibid., 298.
4. Matthew 7:1–5; Luke 6:37–42.
5. John 5:30.
6. Leviticus 19:15.
7. Proverbs 31:9.

CHAPTER 5: Pop Psychology Myth #5:
All Guilt Is Bad

1. Dyer 1976, 91, 89.
2. Ibid., 93.
3. Ibid., 104.
4. Ibid., 103.
5. Ibid., 103.
6. Ibid., 106.
7. Landers 1978, 514–17.
8. 2 Corinthians 7:10.

CHAPTER 6: Pop Psychology Myth #6:
You Need to Think Positively

1. Romans 12:2.
2. Peale 1952, 18.
3. Ibid., 33.
4. Ibid., 24.
5. Ibid., 70.
6. Ibid., 70.
7. Proverbs 23:7.
8. Helmstetter 1982, 51.
9. Ibid., 51.
10. Ibid., 52.
11. Ibid., 52.
12. Ibid., 52.
13. Ibid., 153.
14. Ibid., 44.
15. Ibid., 169.
16. Ibid., 170.
17. Proverbs 23:7.
18. Ecclesiastes 8:14.
19. Jeremiah 17:9.
20. Romans 3:23.
21. 1 Peter 5:8.
22. James 5:1.
23. John 3:16.

24. Philippians 4:19.
25. Romans 8:1.

CHAPTER 7: Pop Psychology Myth #7:
Staying "In Love" Is the Key to a Great Relationship

1. DeAngelis 1987, xv, xvi.
2. Ibid., xv.
3. Ibid., 6–7.
4. Ibid., 14.
5. Ibid., 43.
6. Ibid., 56.
7. Ibid., 63.
8. Ibid., 353–54.
9. Ibid., 370.
10. Genesis 2:24.
11. Matthew 19:6.
12. Ephesians 5:25.
13. 1 Peter 3:7.
14. Matthew 6:7–8.
15. Philippians 4:19
16. 1 Corinthians 13:4–8.

CHAPTER 8: Pop Psychology Myth #8:
You Have Unlimited Power and Potential

1. McGinnis 1979, 20–21.
2. Robbins 1991, 19, 22.
3. Dyer 1980, xv.
4. Ibid., xix.
5. Ibid., 1.
6. Ibid., 2.
7. Ibid., 1.
8. Helmstetter 1982, 194.
9. Genesis 1:27.
10. Hebrews 2:7.
11. Deuteronomy 30:19.
12. Psalm 127:1.
13. Psalm 147:5.

14. Jeremiah 10:12.
15. 2 Chronicles 20:6.
16. 1 Corinthians 1:31.
17. Psalm 44:8.

CHAPTER 9: Pop Psychology Myth #9:
Your Happiness Is the Most Important Thing in Life

1. Piper 1986, 15.
2. Ringer 1977, 7.
3. Ibid., 10.
4. Ibid., 11–12.
5. Ibid., 12.
6. Ibid., 12.
7. Ibid., 14.
8. Ibid., 15.
9. Ibid., 20.
10. Ibid., 20.
11. Ibid., 20.
12. Ibid., 21.
13. Dyer 1976, 15.
14. Ibid., 2.
15. Ibid., 2.
16. Ibid., 17.
17. McWilliams 1991, 423.
18. Piper 1986, 19.
19. Ibid., 19.
20. Myers 1992, 87.
21. Matthew 18:10–14.
22. Esther 8:16.
23. Job 20:20
24. Ecclesiastes 7:14.
25. Ecclesiastes 11:9.
26. Jonah 4:5–10.
27. Ecclesiastes 2:4–10.
28. Ecclesiastes 1:2, 1:8, 1:14, 2:1–2, 2:11, 2:17–19, 2:22–23, 5:10–11.
29. Ecclesiastes 12:13.

30. Piper 1986, 19.
31. Philippians 4:11.
32. Ephesians 4:13.
33. Isaiah 53:3.
34. Piper 1986, 16.
35. Hugo.
36. Shaw 1903.
37. Piper 1986.

CHAPTER 10: Pop Psychology Myth #10:
God Can Be Anything You Want Him to Be

1. Wuthnow 1994, 22.
2. Ibid., 22.
3. Ibid., 23.
4. Playfair 1991, 103.
5. Kaminer 1993, 22.
6. Deuteronomy 29:29.
7. See Genesis 21:33.
8. Sproul 1992, 37.
9. See Isaiah 40:13–14.
10. See Malachi 3:6; James 1:17.
11. See 1 Kings 8:27; Acts 17:24–28.
12. See Leviticus 11:44; John 17:11.
13. See 1 John 4:8.
14. See Genesis 17:1; 2 Corinthians 6:18.
15. See Titus 1:2.
16. See James 1:13.
17. See 2 Timothy 2:13.
18. See Ephesians 1:9.
19. See Job 42:2.
20. See Psalm 139:7–11.
21. Sproul 1992, 43.
22. See Psalm 139:16; Acts 15:18.
23. Tozier 1978, 62–63.
24. See Romans 3:4; Titus 1:2.
25. See Romans 9:15.
26. Psalm 25:8.

27. James 1:17.
28. Romans 8:28.

CONCLUSION: Self-Help or God-Help?

1. Gross 1978, 5.
2. 2 Timothy 4:3.
3. Kaminer 1993, xiii.
4. Ephesians 4:14.
5. James 1:22.
6. Boice 1986, 97.
7. Psalm 121:1.
8. Psalm 121:2.
9. 2 Timothy 3:16–17.
10. Romans 12:10.
11. Romans 12:13.
12. Romans 12:15.
13. Romans 12:16.
14. Romans 12:18.
15. Galatians 6:10.
16. Philippians 4:19.
17. Jeremiah 29:11.
18. Colossians 2:4.
19. Colossians 2:8.

REFERENCES

Beattie, Melody. *Codependent No More*. San Francisco: HarperSan Francisco, 1987.

Boice, James. *Foundations of the Christian Faith*. Downer's Grove, Ill.: Inter-Varsity, 1986.

Brownback, Paul. *The Danger of Self-Love*. Chicago: Moody Press, 1982.

Calvin, John. *Institutes of the Christian Religion*. Translated by Ford L. Battles. Grand Rapids, Mich.: Eerdmans, 1986.

Captain, Phillip. *Eight Stages of Christian Growth*. Englewood Cliffs, N.J.: Prentice Hall, 1984.

Colson, Charles. "The Enduring Revolution: 1993 Templeton Address." Washington, Wilberforce Forum, 1993.

DeAngelis, Barbara. *How to Make Love All the Time*. New York: Dell, 1987.

Dyer, Wayne. *Your Erroneous Zones*. New York: Funk & Wagnalls, 1976.

Dyer, Wayne. *The Sky's the Limit*. New York: Pocket Books, 1980.

Garrison, F. H. *An Introduction to the History of Medicine*. Philadelphia: Saunders, 1921.

Gross, Martin. *The Psychological Society*. New York: Random House, 1978.

Helmstetter, Shad. *What to Say When You Talk to Yourself*. New York: Pocket Books, 1982.

Kaminer, Wendy. *I'm Dysfunctional, You're Dysfunctional*. New York: Vintage Books, 1993.

Landers, Ann. *The Ann Landers Encyclopedia*. New York: Doubleday, 1978.

Maslow, A. *Toward a Psychology of Being*. New York: D. Van Nostrand, 1968.

McGinnis, Alan. *The Friendship Factor*. Minneapolis: Augsburg Publishing House, 1979.

McKay, Matthew, and Patrick Fanning. *Self-Esteem*. New York: St. Martin's Press, 1987.

McWilliams, Peter. *Life 101*. Los Angeles: Prelude Press, 1991.

McWilliams, Peter. *Love 101*. Los Angeles: Prelude Press, 1995.

Menninger, Karl. *Whatever Became of Sin?* New York: Hawthorn, 1973.

Myers, David. *The Pursuit of Happiness*. New York: Avon Books, 1992.

Narramore, Bruce. *You're Someone Special*. Grand Rapids, Mich.: Zondervan, 1978.

Narramore, Bruce, and Bill Counts. *Freedom from Guilt*. Eugene, Ore.: Harvest House, 1974.

Passantino, Bob, and Gretchen Passantino. "Psychology and the Church: Part One—Laying a Foundation for Discernment." *Christian Research Journal*, Winter 1995.

Peale, Norman Vincent. *The Power of Positive Thinking*. New York: Prentice-Hall, 1952.

Piper, John. *Desiring God*. Portland, Ore.: Multnomah, 1986.

Playfair, William. *The Useful Lie*. Wheaton, Ill.: Crossway Books, 1991.

Prager, Dennis. *The Dennis Prager Show*. "Are People Basically Good?" Nov. 22, 1994. Multimedia Entertainment.

Ringer, Robert. *Looking Out for Number One*. New York: Fawcett Crest, 1977.

Robbins, Anthony. *Awaken the Giant Within*. New York: Fireside Books, 1991.

Schwartz, Jackie. *Letting Go of Stress*. New York: Pinnacle, 1982.

Shaw, George Bernard. *Man and Superman*.

Sproul, R. C. *Essential Truths of the Christian Faith*. Wheaton, Ill.: Tyndale House, 1992.

Starker, Steven. *Oracle at the Supermarket*. New Brunswick, N.J.: Transaction Publishers, 1989.

Thurman, Chris. *The Lies We Believe*. Nashville: Thomas Nelson, 1989.

Thurman, Chris. *The Truths We Must Believe*. Nashville: Thomas Nelson, 1991.

Thurman, Chris. *The Lies We Believe Workbook*. Nashville: Thomas Nelson, 1995.

Torrey, E. Fuller. *Freudian Fraud*. New York: HarperCollins, 1992.

Tozier, A. W. *The Knowledge of the Holy*. New York: Harper, 1978.

Trobisch, Walter. *Love Yourself*. Downers Grove, Ill.: Inter-Varsity, 1976.

Vine, W. E., Merrill F. Unger, and William White, Jr. *Vine's Complete Expository Dictionary of Old and New Testament Words*. Nashville: Thomas Nelson, 1946.

Vitz, Paul. *Psychology as Religion: The Cult of Self-Worship*. Grand Rapids, Mich.: Eerdmans, 1977.

Watson, John B. *Psychological Care of Infant and Child*. New York: Norton, 1928.

The Westminster Confession of Faith. Committee for Christian Education and Publication, Presbyterian Church in America, 1990.

Wuthnow, Robert. "How Small Groups Are Transforming Our Lives." *Christianity Today*, 7 February 1994, 20–24.